Better Homes and Gardens®

cookie classics

timeless
family
favorites

Better Homes and Gardens® Books
Des Moines, Iowa

All of us at Better Homes and Gardens® Books are dedicated to providing you with the information and ideas you need to create delicious foods. We welcome your comments and suggestions. Write to us at: Better Homes and Gardens® Books, Cookbook Editorial Department, 1716 Locust St., Des Moines, IA 50309-3023.

If you would like to order additional copies of any of our books, please check with your local bookstore.

 Our seal assures you that every recipe in *Cookie Classics* has been tested in the Better Homes and Gardens® Test Kitchen. This means that each recipe is practical and reliable, and meets our high standards of taste appeal. We guarantee your satisfaction with this book for as long as you own it.

Pictured on front cover (clockwise, beginning with large photograph): Chocolate Ribbon Cookies (*page 71*), Double-Cherry Streusel Bars (*page 24*), Spiral Cookies (*page 75*)

Copyright © 1998 by Meredith Corporation, Des Moines, Iowa.
All rights reserved. Printed in the Hong Kong.
First Edition. Printing Number and Year: 5 4 3 2 1   02 01 00 99 98
Library of Congress Catalog Card Number: 97-75852
ISBN: 0-696-20795-8

Better Homes and Gardens® Books
An imprint of Meredith® Books

Cookie Classics
Editor: Kristi M. Fuller
Contributing Editors: Linda Henry, Shelli McConnell, Mary Williams, Spectrum Communication Services, Inc.
Contributing Writer: David Feder
Associate Art Directors: Lynda Haupert, Ken Carlson
Copy Chief: Catherine Hamrick
Copy and Production Editor: Terri Fredrickson
Contributing Copy Editor: Rosanne Mattson
Contributing Proofreaders: Kathy Eastman, Lisa Green, Martha Long
Indexer: Martha Fifield
Electronic Production Coordinator: Paula Forest
Editorial and Design Assistants: Judy Bailey, Treesa Landry, Karen Schirm
Test Kitchen Director: Sharon Stilwell
Test Kitchen Product Supervisor: Marilyn Cornelius
Photographers: Peter Krumhardt, Andy Lyons, Sandy May
Food Stylists: Dianna Nolin, Glenda Dawson
Production Director: Douglas M. Johnston
Production Manager: Pam Kvitne
Assistant Prepress Manager: Marjorie J. Schenkelberg

Meredith® Books
Editor in Chief: James D. Blume
Design Director: Matt Strelecki
Managing Editor: Gregory H. Kayko
Executive Food Editor: Lisa Holderness

Director, Sales & Marketing, Retail: Michael A. Peterson
Director, Sales & Marketing, Special Markets: Rita McMullen
Director, Sales & Marketing, Home & Garden Center Channel: Ray Wolf
Director, Operations: George A. Susral

Vice President, General Manager: Jamie L. Martin

Better Homes and Gardens® Magazine
Editor in Chief: Jean LemMon
Executive Food Editor: Nancy Byal

Meredith Publishing Group
President, Publishing Group: Christopher M. Little
Vice President, Consumer Marketing & Development: Hal Oringer

Meredith Corporation
Chairman and Chief Executive Officer: William T. Kerr

Chairman of the Executive Committee: E. T. Meredith III

contents

cookie basics

Baking cookies for loved ones warms the heart. For the best cookies ever, follow these practical tips with a dash of your own TLC. Enlist a few helpers—your family or maybe a few neighborhood kids—for an afternoon of cookie creativity and memories in the making.

The following simple tips will ensure top-notch, mouth-watering bars, brownies, and cookies.

test kitchen hints

- **Use fresh ingredients.** If the eggs used aren't fresh or the chocolate is stale, your cookies won't taste fresh. Always start with the best ingredients.
- **Measure accurately.** Use glass measuring cups for liquid ingredients and dry measuring cups for dry ingredients.
- **Mix** all of the ingredients in one bowl. Our recipes have been tested to allow you to skip the traditional step of beating the sugar and butter or shortening together in a separate bowl from the dry ingredients.
- **Stir** in the last of the flour, if using a portable mixer. As you beat in the flour with the mixer, the dough stiffens, making it too difficult to use a portable mixer.
- **Chill dough** in the refrigerator when instructed to do so to make the dough easier to work with.
- **Avoid** using dark cookie sheets. Dark sheets absorb heat and may cause your cookies to overbrown too quickly on the bottom. Shiny, heavy-gauge aluminum sheets work best, as do nonstick cookie sheets if they're not too dark.
- **Preheat** the oven at least 10 minutes before baking.
- **Grease** the cookie sheets only when the recipe instructs you to. Otherwise the cookies may spread too much and become flat.

- **Cool cookie sheet** completely between batches to prevent the cookies from spreading too much.
- **For more even baking,** bake the cookies on the middle rack of the oven.
- **Check for doneness** at the minimum baking time specified in the recipe. Use a kitchen timer to avoid forgetting when you put the cookies in the oven.
- **Remove cookies** from the cookie sheets immediately unless directed otherwise. Some cookies remain on the cookie sheet for a specified amount of time.
- **Transfer hot cookies** to a wire rack for even cooling. Wire racks are best because they can be cleaned easily. Fat or oil in cookies can cause grease spots and can stain wooden racks.

mix now, bake later

Cookie dough can be refrigerated or frozen and baked later. Store dough in the refrigerator in a tightly covered container for up to 1 week or in the freezer for up to 6 months. Thaw frozen dough before baking.

cookie storage know how

If your cookie monsters don't eat your entire stash of cookies in the first day, you'll need to know how to store the cookies so they stay fresh. Follow these tips:

- **Cool cookies** completely before storing. Otherwise, they'll get too soft and will stick together.
- **Store crisp and soft cookies** separately. Use tightly covered containers or sealed plastic bags to prevent humidity from softening crisp cookies and to keep air from drying out soft cookies.
- **Store bar cookies** in either a tightly covered container or in the pan in which they were baked. Cover the pan tightly with plastic wrap or aluminum foil.
- **Restore softness** to soft cookies that have dried out by laying a wedge of raw apple or a slice of bread on a piece of waxed paper and placing it in the container with the cookies. Remove the apple or bread after 24 hours.
- **For short-term storage,** keep wrapped cookies at room temperature for up to 3 days. Cookies with cream cheese or yogurt in the frosting should be refrigerated.
- **For long-term storage,** freeze cookies in a freezer-safe container or plastic bag for up to 12 months. To serve, thaw cookies 10 to 15 minutes at room temperature.

cookies: special delivery

Send a care package to those you love who live far away. Have the cookies delivered unharmed using these hints:

- **Choose sturdy cookies** that will travel well. Most bar or soft, moist cookies are good choices. But frosting or filling on some cookies may soften, causing them to stick together or to the wrapping.
- **Wrap cookies** in pairs, back to back, or individually with plastic wrap.
- **Choose a heavy box** and line it with plastic wrap or foil. Place a generous layer of filler, such as plastic bubble wrap; foam packing pieces; or crumpled tissue paper, paper towels, waxed paper or brown paper bags, on the bottom of the box.
- **Layer the cookies** and the filler. End with plenty of filler to prevent the contents from shifting during shipping.

ingredient smarts

Using the right ingredients is as important as using fresh ingredients. Follow these tips for both:

- **Eggs.** All recipes in this cookbook were tested using large eggs. Store eggs in the egg carton for up to 5 weeks after the packing date printed on the carton. Or, check for a "use by" date on the carton.
- **Flour.** Most of the recipes in this cookbook use all-purpose flour, although a few may include some whole wheat flour. Store both types of flour in sealed plastic bags or transfer them to airtight storage containers; keep in a cool, dry place. All-purpose flour will stay fresh 10 to 15 months; whole grain flour will stay fresh for up to 5 months.
- **Sugars.** When a recipe calls for sugar, use white granulated sugar. Powdered sugar or confectioners' sugar refers to granulated sugar that has been pulverized; cornstarch is often added to prevent caking. It usually is sifted *before* measuring. Brown sugar is a mix of granulated sugar and molasses; the amount of molasses determines whether the sugar is light or dark. Transfer sugars that are bought in boxes to a sealed plastic bag or an airtight container. Stored in a cool, dry place, sugars will keep indefinitely.
- **Baking powder and baking soda.** Both are important to baking, making cookies rise and become light. Store in an airtight container in a cool, dry place. For best results, replace every 6 months or check the "use by" date.

classic

chocolate chip cookies

prep: 25 minutes   **bake:** 8 minutes   **oven:** 375°

Nothing beats a classic. Chocolate chip cookies were probably the first cookies you ever baked. This recipe is an updated version that first appeared in the 1941 edition of the Better Homes and Gardens® cookbook.

½ cup shortening
½ cup butter
½ cup granulated sugar
 1 cup packed brown sugar
½ teaspoon baking soda
 2 eggs

 1 teaspoon vanilla
2½ cups all-purpose flour
 1 12-ounce package (2 cups) semisweet
      chocolate pieces
1½ cups chopped walnuts, pecans, or
      hazelnuts (filberts) (optional)

1. In a large mixing bowl beat the shortening and butter with an electric mixer on medium to high speed for 30 seconds. Add the granulated sugar, brown sugar, and baking soda. Beat mixture until combined, scraping sides of bowl occasionally. Beat in the eggs and vanilla until combined. Beat in as much of the flour as you can with the mixer. Stir in remaining flour. Stir in chocolate pieces and, if desired, nuts.

2. Drop dough by rounded teaspoons 2 inches apart onto an ungreased cookie sheet.

3. Bake cookies in a 375° oven for 8 to 10 minutes or until edges are lightly browned. Transfer cookies to a wire rack; cool. Makes about 60 cookies.

Nutrition Facts per cookie: 99 calories, 5 g total fat (1 g saturated fat), 11 mg cholesterol, 29 mg sodium, 12 g carbohydrate, 0 g fiber, 1 g protein.

classics

When it comes to cookies, nothing beats the good old-fashioned kind that Grandma lovingly put in her cookie jar. Find your favorites here.

ranger cookies

prep: 25 minutes   **bake:** 8 minutes   **oven:** 375°

Whether you're hiking in a state park or picnicking in your own backyard, a hearty mix of crisped rice, oats, and dates makes this cookie a camper's treat.

½ cup butter
½ cup granulated sugar
½ cup packed brown sugar
½ teaspoon baking powder
¼ teaspoon baking soda
1 egg

1 teaspoon vanilla
1¼ cups all-purpose flour
2 cups crisp rice cereal or 1 cup rolled oats
1 3½-ounce can (1⅓ cups) flaked coconut
1 cup snipped pitted whole dates or raisins

1. In a medium mixing bowl beat the butter with an electric mixer for 30 seconds. Add the granulated sugar, brown sugar, baking powder, and baking soda; beat until combined. Beat in the egg and vanilla. Beat in as much of the flour as you can with the mixer. Stir in remaining flour. Stir in cereal or oats, coconut, and dates or raisins.

2. Drop dough by a rounded teaspoon 2 inches apart onto an ungreased cookie sheet.

3. Bake cookies in a 375° oven about 8 minutes or until edges are golden brown. Cool on cookie sheet for 1 minute. Transfer to a wire rack; cool. Makes about 54 cookies.

Nutrition Facts per cookie: 61 calories, 2 g total fat (2 g saturated fat), 8 mg cholesterol, 40 mg sodium, 10 g carbohydrate, 1 g fiber, 1 g protein.

baking in thin air

The higher the altitude, the more difficulty you may have getting your cookies to come out perfectly. Although more stable than cakes, cookie recipes may need to be adjusted a little. Here are a few tricks to help ensure your cookies won't suffer too badly from that Rocky Mountain high.

- Increase the oven temperature by 25° and slightly decrease the baking time (try 1 to 2 minutes).
- You may need to reduce the sugar slightly (try just a couple of tablespoons to start).
- If a recipe calls for baking powder or soda, you may need to reduce the amount (try ⅛ teaspoon less).

toasted oatmeal cookies

prep: 25 minutes   **bake:** 10 minutes   **oven:** 375°

Give your old-fashioned iced oatmeal cookies a nutty richness by browning the rolled oats slightly in the oven before using. If you like, toast a batch of oatmeal ahead and keep it on hand in an airtight container.

1½ cups regular rolled oats	½ teaspoon salt
⅓ cup buttermilk or sour milk	2 eggs
2 cups packed brown sugar	1 teaspoon vanilla
¾ cup shortening	2½ cups all-purpose flour
1 teaspoon baking powder	1 cup chopped pitted dates
1 teaspoon baking soda	1 cup chopped walnuts or pecans
1 teaspoon ground cinnamon	1 recipe Powdered Sugar Icing (optional)
1 teaspoon ground nutmeg	

1. Sprinkle oats in a shallow baking pan. Bake oats in a 375° oven about 10 minutes or until lightly toasted, stirring once. Meanwhile, grease a cookie sheet; set aside.

2. Place the toasted oats in a small bowl. Stir in buttermilk or sour milk and let stand a few minutes.

3. In a medium mixing bowl beat together the brown sugar and shortening with an electric mixer on medium to high speed until combined. Add the baking powder, baking soda, cinnamon, nutmeg, and salt; beat until combined. Beat in eggs and vanilla. Stir in the oat mixture.

4. Beat in as much of the flour as you can with the mixer. Stir in dates, nuts, and remaining flour. Drop dough by a rounded teaspoon 2 inches apart onto prepared cookie sheet.

5. Bake cookies in a 375° oven about 10 minutes or until edges are golden brown. Transfer cookies to a wire rack; cool. If desired, drizzle with Powdered Sugar Icing. Makes about 60 cookies.

Powdered Sugar Icing: Combine 1 cup sifted powdered sugar, ¼ teaspoon vanilla, and enough milk (2 to 4 teaspoons) to make of drizzling consistency.

Nutrition Facts per cookie: 100 calories, 4 g total fat (1 g saturated fat), 7 mg cholesterol, 52 mg sodium, 15 g carbohydrate, 0 g fiber, 1 g protein.

pecan snaps with espresso cream

prep: 35 minutes **bake:** 8 minutes **oven:** 350°

Dress up a special occasion or party with these coffee-and-cream-filled cookies. They're elegant and sumptuous.

¼ cup packed brown sugar	3 ounces semisweet chocolate, melted
3 tablespoons butter, melted	(optional)
2 tablespoons dark-colored corn syrup	1 cup whipping cream
1 tablespoon coffee liqueur or coffee	¼ cup sifted powdered sugar
½ cup very finely chopped pecans	4 teaspoons instant espresso coffee powder
¼ cup all-purpose flour	Grated chocolate (optional)

1. Lightly grease a cookie sheet or line with foil. In a small bowl stir together brown sugar, melted butter, corn syrup, and coffee liqueur or coffee. Stir in pecans and flour until combined. Drop batter by a level teaspoon 3 inches apart, or a level tablespoon 5 inches apart, onto the prepared cookie sheet. (Bake only 4 or 5 cookies at a time.) Bake in a 350° oven for 7 to 8 minutes for smaller cookies or 8 to 10 minutes for larger cookies or until cookies are bubbly and a deep golden brown.

2. Cool cookies on the cookie sheet for 1 to 2 minutes or until set. Quickly remove 1 cookie; roll cookie around a metal cone or the greased handle of a wooden spoon (see photos, *below*). When the cookie is firm, slide the cookie off the cone or spoon and cool completely on a wire rack. Repeat with remaining cookies, 1 at a time. (If cookies harden before you can shape them, reheat them in the oven about 1 minute or until softened.) If desired,

carefully brush the top edge of each cone with melted semisweet chocolate. (Use a light touch, as the cookies are fragile and will break.)

3. Up to 30 minutes before serving, in a large mixing bowl beat whipping cream, powdered sugar, and espresso coffee powder with an electric mixer on low speed until stiff peaks form. Pipe or spoon some of the whipped cream into each cookie. If desired, sprinkle with grated chocolate. Makes about 30 small or 11 large cookies.

To make ahead: Bake, shape, and cool cookies as directed. Arrange in a single layer in a freezer container and freeze for up to 1 month. To serve, thaw cookies for 15 minutes. Prepare the whipped cream mixture and fill the cookies as directed.

Nutrition Facts per small cookie: 68 calories, 5 g total fat
(3 g saturated fat), 14 mg cholesterol, 16 mg sodium,
5 g carbohydrate, 0 g fiber, 0 g protein.

snickerdoodles

prep: 25 minutes   **bake:** 10 minutes   **oven:** 375°

Few other cookies appeal more to kids. Snickerdoodles—the very name a promise of fun—are simple to make. Wherever the name originated, it's certain that these cookies will become favorites.

½ cup butter
1 cup sugar
¼ teaspoon baking soda
¼ teaspoon cream of tartar
1 egg

½ teaspoon vanilla
1½ cups all-purpose flour
2 tablespoons sugar
1 teaspoon ground cinnamon

1. In a medium mixing bowl beat the butter with an electric mixer on medium to high speed for 30 seconds. Add the 1 cup sugar, baking soda, and cream of tartar. Beat until combined, scraping sides of bowl. Beat in the egg and vanilla. Beat in as much of the flour as you can with the mixer. Stir in remaining flour. Cover dough and chill in the refrigerator for 1 hour.

2. In a small mixing bowl combine the 2 tablespoons sugar and the cinnamon. Shape dough into 1-inch balls. Roll balls in the sugar-cinnamon mixture to coat. Place 2 inches apart on an ungreased cookie sheet.

3. Bake the cookies in a 375° oven for 10 to 11 minutes or until edges are golden brown. Transfer cookies to a wire rack; cool. Makes about 36 cookies.

Nutrition Facts per cookie: 66 calories, 3 g total fat (2 g saturated fat), 13 mg cholesterol, 36 mg sodium, 10 g carbohydrate, 0 g fiber, 1 g protein.

from the flour bin

Too much flour added to a cookie recipe can cause the cookies to turn into hard rocks. Too little and you end up with flat pancakes. To ensure that you add the correct amount of flour, measure carefully.

- Stir the flour prior to measuring. Flour settles as it sits and if you don't stir it, you may end up adding too much flour to your cookies.
- Spoon the flour into the measuring cup. Resist the urge to dip the measuring cup into the flour. Dipping, which packs the flour as you dip, will result in adding too much flour.
- Level it off with the edge of a knife. Mounds of flour above the cup result in too much flour.

gingersnaps

prep: 25 minutes   **bake:** 8 minutes   **oven:** 375°

To make their gingersnaps snappier, Southern bakers like to add a pinch or two of ground black pepper to the dough. Try it with your next batch.

¾   cup shortening
1   cup packed brown sugar
1   teaspoon baking soda
1   teaspoon ground ginger
1   teaspoon ground cinnamon

½   teaspoon ground cloves
¼   cup light-flavored molasses
1   egg
2¼ cups all-purpose flour
¼   cup granulated sugar

1. In a large mixing bowl beat shortening with an electric mixer on medium to high speed for 30 seconds. Add the brown sugar, baking soda, ginger, cinnamon, and cloves. Beat on medium to high speed until combined. Beat in molasses and egg. Beat in as much of the flour as you can with the mixer. Stir in remaining flour.

2. Shape dough into 1-inch balls. Roll balls in the granulated sugar to coat. Place balls 2 inches apart on an ungreased cookie sheet.

3. Bake cookies in a 375° oven for 8 to 10 minutes or until the edges are set and the tops are slightly cracked. Cool cookies on the cookie sheet for 1 minute. Transfer cookies to a wire rack; cool. Makes about 48 cookies.

Nutrition Facts per cookie: 72 calories, 3 g total fat (1 g saturated fat), 4 mg cholesterol, 29 mg sodium, 10 g carbohydrate, 0 g fiber, 1 g protein

pizzelles

prep: 15 minutes   **bake:** 2 minutes

The pizzelle (peets-TSEH-leh)—one of the oldest cookie recipes known—is a large, crisp Italian cookie. The cookies are made with a pizzelle iron, which is similar to a waffle iron but more intricately designed. You can either buy an electric pizzelle iron or one that is heated on the rangetop.

2 cups all-purpose flour	3 eggs
1 tablespoon baking powder	¾ cup sugar
1½ teaspoons ground nutmeg	⅓ cup butter, melted and cooled
½ teaspoon ground cardamom	2 teaspoons vanilla

1. In a medium mixing bowl stir together the flour, baking powder, nutmeg, and cardamom; set aside. In a small mixing bowl beat the eggs with an electric mixer on high speed about 4 minutes or until thick and lemon-colored. Using medium speed, gradually beat in the sugar.

2. Beat in the cooled butter and the vanilla. Add flour mixture; beat on low speed until combined.

3. Heat electric pizzelle iron according to manufacturer's directions. (Or, heat pizzelle iron on range top over medium heat until a drop of water sizzles on the grid. Reduce heat to medium-low.)

4. For each pizzelle, place a slightly rounded tablespoon of batter on pizzelle iron, slightly off-center toward back of grid (see photos, *below*). Close lid. Bake according to manufacturer's directions. (For a nonelectric iron, bake about 2 minutes or until golden brown, turning once.) Turn pizzelles out onto a paper towel to cool. Repeat with remaining batter. Makes 18 pizzelles.

Nutrition Facts per pizzelle: 125 calories, 5 g total fat (1 g saturated fat), 40 mg cholesterol, 102 mg sodium, 19 g carbohydrate, 0 g fiber, 2 g protein.

crackled sugar cookies

prep: 25 minutes **bake:** 20 minutes **oven:** 300°

It's a different kind of sugar cookie, slow-baked to sweet perfection, with a surface crackled like the moon.

½ cup butter
½ cup shortening
2 cups granulated sugar
1 teaspoon baking soda
1 teaspoon cream of tartar

⅛ teaspoon salt
3 egg yolks
½ teaspoon vanilla
2 cups all-purpose flour

1. In a large mixing bowl beat the butter and shortening with an electric mixer on medium to high speed for 30 seconds. Add the sugar, baking soda, cream of tartar, and salt. Beat until combined. Beat in the egg yolks and vanilla. Beat in as much of the flour as you can with the mixer. Stir in remaining flour.

2. Shape dough into 1-inch balls. Place 2 inches apart on an ungreased cookie sheet.

3. Bake cookies in a 300° oven about 20 minutes or until tops are slightly cracked and sides are set (do not let edges brown). Transfer cookies to a wire rack; cool. Makes about 48 cookies.

Nutrition Facts per cookie: 90 calories, 5 g total fat
(1 g saturated fat), 16 mg cholesterol, 50 mg sodium,
12 g carbohydrate, 0 g fiber, 1 g protein.

child's play

Cookies are a great way to introduce children to the joys of baking. But a kitchen is not a playground. Observe these safety steps when using your kitchen as a classroom:

• Supervise children in any step that involves dangerous equipment, such as a mixer, knives, the rangetop, and the oven.
• Keep plenty of towels handy for spills.
• Review each step before baking, laying out the ingredients and equipment you'll be using.
• Clean as you go to set the best example for your budding bakers.

peanut butter cookies

prep: 25 minutes   **bake:** 7 minutes   **oven:** 325°

Old-fashioned peanut butter cookies are a long-time favorite. Keep your cookie jar filled so you have some on hand for after-school snacks or as generous rewards for chores well done.

½ cup butter
½ cup peanut butter
½ cup granulated sugar
½ cup packed brown sugar or ¼ cup honey
½ teaspoon baking soda

½ teaspoon baking powder
1 egg
½ teaspoon vanilla
1½ cups all-purpose flour
    Granulated sugar

1. In a large mixing bowl beat the butter and peanut butter with an electric mixer on medium to high speed for 30 seconds. Add the granulated sugar, brown sugar or honey, baking soda, and baking powder. Beat until combined, scraping sides of bowl occasionally. Beat in the egg and vanilla. Beat in as much of the flour as you can with the mixer. Stir in remaining flour. (If necessary, cover and chill dough in refrigerator until easy to handle.)

2. Shape dough into 2-inch balls. Roll in additional granulated sugar to coat. Place balls 2 inches apart on an ungreased cookie sheet. Flatten by making crisscross marks with the tines of a fork.

3. Bake cookies in a 375° oven for 7 to 9 minutes or until bottoms of cookies are lightly browned. Transfer cookies to a wire rack; cool. Makes about 36 cookies.

Nutrition Facts per cookie: 83 calories, 4 g total fat
(2 g saturated fat), 13 mg cholesterol, 68 mg sodium,
10 g carbohydrate, 0 g fiber, 1 g protein.

malted milk cookies

prep: 20 minutes   **bake:** 10 minutes   **oven:** 375°

You'll be reminded of a creamy old-fashioned malt every time you take a bite of these chocolate cookies.

1 cup butter
¾ cup granulated sugar
¾ cup packed brown sugar
1 teaspoon baking soda
2 eggs
1 teaspoon vanilla

2 ounces unsweetened chocolate, melted
    and cooled
2¼ cups all-purpose flour
½ cup instant malted milk powder
1 cup coarsely chopped malted
    milk balls

1. In a large mixing bowl beat the butter with an electric mixer on medium to high speed for 30 seconds. Add the granulated sugar, brown sugar, and baking soda. Beat mixture until combined, scraping sides of bowl occasionally. Beat in the eggs, vanilla, and melted chocolate until combined. Beat in as much of the flour as you can with the mixer. Stir in remaining flour and the malted milk powder. Stir in the malted milk balls.

2. Drop dough from a rounded teaspoon 2½ inches apart on an ungreased cookie sheet. Bake in a 375° oven about 10 minutes or until edges are firm. Cool on cookie sheet for 1 minute. Transfer cookies to a wire rack; cool. Makes about 36 cookies.

Nutrition Facts per cookie: 138 calories, 7 g total fat
(4 g saturated fat), 26 mg cholesterol, 112 mg sodium,
18 g carbohydrate, 0 g fiber, 2 g protein.

being exact

Ever wonder how you can always end up with the right amount of cookies as the recipe indicates? As long as you don't sample too much cookie dough (especially since cookies generally contain raw eggs, which aren't considered safe to eat anyway), you can ensure that you get the right amount every time if you follow this tip.

Pat the dough into a square. Cut the square of dough into the number of pieces the recipe should yield. If you want 48 cookies, for example, cut the dough into six equal strips in one direction and eight equal strips the other direction. Shape the cut pieces into 48 balls and place them on the cookie sheet.

spiced apple drops

prep: 20 minutes   **bake:** 10 minutes   **oven:** 375°

Apples, spice, and everything nice—that's what these cookies are made of. The buttery apple frosting makes them an extra-special treat. To keep them fresh, store the frosted cookies in a covered container in the refrigerator.

½ cup butter	1 egg
⅔ cup granulated sugar	¼ cup apple juice or apple cider
⅔ cup brown sugar	2 cups all-purpose flour
1 teaspoon ground cinnamon	1 cup finely chopped apple
½ teaspoon baking soda	1 cup chopped walnuts
½ teaspoon ground nutmeg	1 recipe Apple Frosting
⅛ teaspoon ground cloves	

1. Lightly grease a cookie sheet. Set aside. In a large mixing bowl beat the butter with an electric mixer on medium to high speed for 30 seconds. Add the granulated sugar, brown sugar, cinnamon, baking soda, nutmeg, and cloves. Beat until combined, scraping the sides of bowl. Beat in the egg and apple juice or cider until combined. Beat in as much of the flour as you can with the mixer. Stir in remaining flour, the apple, and walnuts. Drop dough by a rounded teaspoon 2 inches apart onto prepared cookie sheet.

2. Bake cookies in a 375° oven for 10 to 12 minutes or until edges are lightly browned. Cool on cookie sheet for 1 minute. Transfer cookies to a wire rack; cool. Spread with Apple Frosting. Makes about 40 cookies.

Apple Frosting: In a medium mixing bowl beat 4 cups sifted powdered sugar, ¼ cup softened butter, 1 teaspoon vanilla, and 3 to 4 tablespoons apple juice to make a frosting of spreading consistency.

Nutrition Facts per cookie: 138 calories, 5 g total fat (2 g saturated fat), 15 mg cholesterol, 54 mg sodium, 22 g carbohydrate, 0 g fiber, 1 g protein.

best bars

turtle shortbread bars

prep: 20 minutes **bake:** 15 minutes/25 minutes **cool:** 10 minutes **oven:** 350°

The original turtles—chocolate-covered caramel and pecan candies—were so named because they were shaped like turtles. These bars contain all the goodies of a turtle—with the addition of coconut—on top of a shortbread base.

1 cup all-purpose flour	2 cups coarsely chopped pecans
½ cup packed brown sugar	1 cup flaked coconut
½ cup butter	20 vanilla caramels, unwrapped
1 14-ounce can (1¼ cups) sweetened condensed milk	2 tablespoons milk
2 teaspoons vanilla	1 cup milk chocolate pieces or semisweet chocolate pieces

1. For crust, in a medium mixing bowl stir together the flour and brown sugar. Using a pastry blender, cut in the butter until the mixture resembles coarse crumbs.

2. Press crumb mixture into the bottom of an ungreased 13x9x2-inch baking pan. Bake crust in a 350° oven for 15 minutes.

3. Meanwhile, for filling, combine sweetened condensed milk and vanilla. Sprinkle pecans and coconut over partially baked crust. Pour filling over pecans and coconut.

4. Bake bars for 25 to 30 minutes more or until filling is set. Cool on a wire rack for 10 minutes.

5. In a small saucepan combine caramels and milk. Cook and stir over medium-low heat just until caramels are melted. Drizzle caramel mixture over filling. Sprinkle with chocolate pieces. Cool completely. Cut into bars. Makes 48 bars.

Nutrition Facts per bar: 132 calories, 8 g total fat (2 g saturated fat), 6 mg cholesterol, 42 mg sodium, 15 g carbohydrate, 1 g fiber, 2 g protein.

& brownies

Bar cookies or brownies are the easiest of all cookies to make. Spread 'em in a pan, bake 'em, and cut 'em into squares. Finishing touches, such as chocolate drizzles, give them personalities all their own.

raspberry cheesecake bars

prep: 25 minutes   **bake:** 12 minutes/15 minutes   **chill:** 3 hours   **oven:** 350°

All the intense flavor of a lavish cheesecake resides in these almond and berry cheesecake bars.

1¼ cups all-purpose flour
½ cup packed brown sugar
½ cup finely chopped, sliced almonds
½ cup butter-flavored shortening or shortening
2 8-ounce packages cream cheese, softened
⅔ cup sugar

2 eggs
¾ teaspoon almond extract
1 cup seedless raspberry preserves or other preserves or jam
½ cup flaked coconut
½ cup sliced almonds

1. In a medium mixing bowl combine flour, brown sugar, and the ½ cup finely chopped almonds. Using a pastry blender, cut in shortening until mixture resembles fine crumbs. Set aside ½ cup crumb mixture for topping.

2. For crust, press remaining crumb mixture into the bottom of an ungreased 13x9x2-inch baking pan. Bake crust in a 350° oven for 12 to 15 minutes or until the edges are golden brown.

3. Meanwhile, in another mixing bowl beat the cream cheese, sugar, eggs, and almond extract with an electric mixer on low to medium speed until smooth. Spread cream cheese mixture over the hot crust. Return to oven and bake 15 minutes more.

4. Stir preserves until smooth. Spread over cream cheese mixture. In a small mixing bowl combine the reserved crumb mixture, the coconut, and sliced almonds. Sprinkle evenly over the preserves.

5. Bake about 15 minutes more or until topping is golden brown. Cool in pan on a wire rack. Cover; chill in the refrigerator for at least 3 hours before cutting into bars. Store the bars, covered, in the refrigerator. Makes 32 bars.

Nutrition Facts per bar: 180 calories, 11 g total fat
(5 g saturated fat), 29 mg cholesterol, 49 mg sodium,
20 g carbohydrate, 1 g fiber, 3 g protein.

macadamia nut bars

prep: 20 minutes   **bake:** 12 minutes/20 minutes   **oven:** 350°

For a taste of the islands, try the optional rum with macadamia nuts. If a Southern flavor is more to your taste, use bourbon and pecans instead.

1¼ cups all-purpose flour
½ cup packed brown sugar
½ teaspoon baking powder
½ cup butter
 3 slightly beaten eggs
¼ cup light-colored corn syrup

½ cup granulated sugar
½ cup packed brown sugar
¼ cup butter, melted
 2 tablespoons rum or bourbon* (optional)
1½ teaspoons vanilla
1½ cups chopped macadamia nuts or pecans*

1. For crust, in a medium mixing bowl stir together the flour, ½ cup brown sugar, and baking powder. Using a pastry blender, cut in the ½ cup butter until mixture resembles coarse crumbs.

2. Press the crust mixture into the bottom of an ungreased 13x9x2-inch baking pan. Bake the crust in a 350° oven for 12 minutes.

3. Meanwhile, for filling, stir together the eggs, corn syrup, granulated sugar, ½ cup brown sugar, the melted butter, rum or bourbon (if desired), and vanilla. Stir in nuts. Pour filling over baked crust, spreading evenly.

4. Bake for 20 to 25 minutes more or until set. Cool on a wire rack. Cut into bars. Makes 32 bars.

Nutrition Facts per bar: 146 calories, 9 g total fat
(3 g saturated fat), 31 mg cholesterol, 59 mg sodium,
15 g carbohydrate, 1 g fiber, 2 g protein.

Note: If using rum, use macadamia nuts. If using bourbon, use pecans.

nuts about nuts

Nuts add such a unique taste and texture to cookies that you'll want to get the best out of them.

- Store unopened packages in a cool, dark place.
- Keep opened packages of nuts in an airtight container in the refrigerator for up to six months or in the freezer for up to one year.
- To remove skins from nuts, such as almonds and hazelnuts (filberts), toast the nuts lightly, then rub with a clean dish towel.
- Feel free to vary nuts in recipes. In a pinch, substitute walnuts for pecans or almonds for hazelnuts.

double-cherry streusel bars

prep: 20 minutes **bake:** 12 minutes/20 minutes **oven:** 350°

This is one fruit-and-nut bar that doesn't skimp on the fruit. If you can't choose between the cherries or the cranberries, use half of each.

2 cups water	1 cup butter
1 cup dried tart cherries or dried cranberries, snipped	½ cup coarsely chopped slivered almonds
2 cups quick-cooking rolled oats	2 12-ounce jars cherry preserves
1½ cups all-purpose flour	1 teaspoon finely shredded lemon peel
1½ cups packed brown sugar	½ cup semisweet chocolate pieces
1 teaspoon baking powder	1 teaspoon shortening, melted
½ teaspoon baking soda	

1. In a small saucepan bring water to boiling. Remove from heat. Add dried cherries or cranberries and let stand 10 minutes or until softened. Drain and set aside.

2. For crust, in a large mixing bowl combine the oats, flour, brown sugar, baking powder, and baking soda. Using a pastry blender, cut in the butter until the mixture resembles coarse crumbs. Reserve 1 cup of the crumb mixture. Stir the almonds into the reserved crumb mixture; set aside.

3. Press remaining crumb mixture into the bottom of an ungreased 15x10x1-inch baking pan. Bake crust in a 350° oven for 12 minutes.

4. Meanwhile, for the filling, stir together the drained cherries, cherry preserves, and lemon peel. Spread the filling evenly over baked crust; sprinkle with reserved crumb mixture (see photos, *below*). Bake bars for 20 to 25 minutes more or until top is golden brown. Cool on a wire rack.

5. In a small saucepan combine the chocolate pieces and shortening; heat over medium-low heat until chocolate is melted. Drizzle melted chocolate mixture over baked bars. Cut into bars. Makes 48 bars.

Nutrition Facts per bar: 144 calories, 5 g total fat
(2 g saturated fat), 10 mg cholesterol, 63 mg sodium,
24 g carbohydrate, 1 g fiber, 1 g protein.

lemon bars deluxe

prep: 20 minutes **bake:** 20 minutes/25 minutes **oven:** 350°

This recipe makes a big batch of these tangy lemon treats so you have plenty to serve hungry guests.

- 2 cups all-purpose flour
- ½ cup sifted powdered sugar
- 1 cup butter
- 4 beaten eggs
- 1½ cups granulated sugar
- 1 to 2 teaspoons finely shredded lemon peel
- ⅓ cup lemon juice
- ¼ cup all-purpose flour
- ½ teaspoon baking powder
- Powdered sugar (optional)

1. In a medium mixing bowl stir together the 2 cups flour and the ½ cup powdered sugar. Using a pastry blender, cut in the butter until mixture clings together. Press into the bottom of an ungreased 13x9x2-inch baking pan.

2. Bake crust in a 350° oven for 20 to 25 minutes or until lightly browned.

3. Meanwhile, beat together the eggs, granulated sugar, and lemon juice. Combine the ¼ cup flour and the baking powder; stir into the egg mixture along with the lemon peel. Pour over the baked crust.

4. Bake bars in a 350° oven for 25 minutes more. Cool on a wire rack. Sift additional powdered sugar over the top of bars. Cut into bars or into 2x1¾-inch diamonds (see page 31). Store bars, covered, in the refrigerator. Makes 30 bars.

Nutrition Facts per bar: 141 calories, 7 g total fat (4 g saturated fat), 45 mg cholesterol, 77 mg sodium, 19 g carbohydrate, 0 g fiber, 2 g protein.

check the size

The correct size baking pan is a must when making bar cookies. You can substitute two 9x9x2-inch pans for a 15x10x1-inch pan or two 8x8x2 inch pans for a 13x9x2-inch pan. Keep the oven temperature the same, but subtract 5 minutes from the baking time.

chocolate-peanut butter bars

prep: 20 minutes   **bake:** 15 minutes/12 minutes   **oven:** 350°

Chocolate and peanut butter have been getting together for years, but never before so sweetly.

2 cups quick-cooking rolled oats	1 12-ounce package (2 cups) semisweet
1¾ cups packed brown sugar	chocolate pieces
1 cup all-purpose flour	1 beaten egg
½ cup whole wheat flour	1 14-ounce can (1¼ cups) sweetened
1 teaspoon baking powder	condensed milk or low-fat sweetened
½ teaspoon baking soda	condensed milk
1 cup butter	⅓ cup creamy peanut butter
½ cup chopped peanuts	

1. For crumb mixture, in a large mixing bowl combine rolled oats, brown sugar, all-purpose flour, whole wheat flour, baking powder, and baking soda. Using a pastry blender, cut in the butter until mixture resembles fine crumbs. Stir in peanuts.

2. For topping, combine 1¾ cups of the crumb mixture and the chocolate pieces; set aside.

3. For crust, stir the egg into remaining crumb mixture. Press into bottom of an ungreased 15x10x1-inch baking pan. Bake in a 350° oven for 15 minutes.

4. For filling, stir together the sweetened condensed milk and peanut butter until smooth. Pour filling evenly over partially baked crust. Sprinkle topping evenly over filling. Bake for 12 to 15 minutes more or until lightly browned around the edges. Cool on a wire rack. Cut into bars. Makes 48 bars.

Nutrition Facts per bar: 163 calories, 9 g total fat
(3 g saturated fat), 17 mg cholesterol, 82 mg sodium,
21 g carbohydrate, 1 g fiber, 3 g protein.

cranberry-pecan bars

prep: 25 minutes   **bake:** 25 minutes   **oven:** 350°

Take your pick of a cranberry-studded bar or the traditional date bar. Either way, they won't last long.

½ cup butter
½ cup packed brown sugar
½ teaspoon baking powder
¼ teaspoon baking soda
1 teaspoon finely shredded orange peel

½ cup orange juice
1 egg
1 cup all-purpose flour
½ cup chopped pecans
½ cup snipped dried cranberries
   Powdered Sugar

1. In a medium mixing bowl beat butter with an electric mixer on medium to high speed about 30 seconds. Add brown sugar, baking powder, and baking soda. Beat in the egg and orange juice on low speed until combined. Beat in as much of the flour as you can. Stir in the orange peel, pecans, cranberries, and remaining flour.

2. Spread batter into an ungreased 11x7x1½-inch baking pan. Bake in a 350° oven about 25 minutes or until a wooden toothpick inserted near the center comes out clean. Cool on a wire rack. Sift powdered sugar over the top. Cut into bars. Makes 24 bars.

Date-Walnut Bars
Prepare Cranberry-Pecan Bars as directed, except substitute ½ cup chopped walnuts for the pecans and ½ cup chopped pitted dates for the cranberries.

Nutrition Facts per bar: 94 calories, 6 g total fat
(3 g saturated fat), 19 mg cholesterol, 64 mg sodium,
11 g carbohydrate, 0 g fiber, 1 g protein.

four-way fudge brownies

prep: 15 minutes **bake:** 30 minutes **oven:** 350°

We couldn't resist improvising on a classic winner. Choose from four different brownies to satisfy everyone's personal craving. For the pure at heart, we've included the basic brownie. (Crème de Menthe Fudge Brownies, pictured.)

- ½ cup butter
- 2 ounces unsweetened chocolate, cut up
- 1 cup sugar
- 2 eggs
- 1 teaspoon vanilla
- ⅔ cup all-purpose flour

1. Grease a 8x8x2-inch baking pan; set aside. In a heavy, medium saucepan, melt butter and chocolate over low heat. Remove from heat. Stir in sugar, eggs, and vanilla. Beat lightly by hand just until combined. Stir in flour.

2. Spread batter into prepared pan. Bake brownies in a 350° oven for 30 minutes. Cool on a wire rack. Cut into triangles or squares. Makes 16 to 20 brownies.

Nutrition Facts per Fudge Brownie: 146 calories, 9 g total fat (2 g saturated fat), 34 mg cholesterol, 61 mg sodium, 17 g carbohydrate, 0 g fiber, 2 g protein.

Crème de Menthe Fudge Brownies

Prepare brownies as directed. Stir ¼ teaspoon mint extract into batter. Bake as directed. For frosting, in a medium bowl beat ¼ cup butter until fluffy. Gradually add 1 cup sifted powdered sugar, beating well. Beat in 2 tablespoons green crème de menthe. Gradually beat in about ½ cup additional sifted powdered sugar to make of spreading consistency. Spread frosting over brownies. Melt 1 ounce semisweet chocolate over low heat; drizzle chocolate over brownies.

Nutrition Facts per Crème de Menthe Fudge Brownie: 224 calories, 12 g total fat (4 g saturated fat), 38 mg cholesterol, 87 mg sodium, 29 g carbohydrate, 0 g fiber, 2 g protein.

Fudge Brownies with Peanut Butter Frosting

Prepare, bake, and cool brownies as directed. For frosting, in a medium mixing bowl beat ¼ cup peanut butter with an electric mixer on low speed until fluffy. Gradually add 1 cup sifted powdered sugar, beating well. Beat in ¼ cup milk and 1 teaspoon vanilla. Gradually beat in about ½ cup additional sifted powdered sugar to make of spreading consistency. Spread frosting over brownies; sprinkle with ¼ cup finely chopped peanuts.

Nutrition Facts per Fudge Brownie with Peanut Butter Frosting: 222 calories, 12 g total fat (3 g saturated fat), 34 mg cholesterol, 92 mg sodium, 28 g carbohydrate, 1 g fiber, 3 g protein.

Caramel Nut Fudge Brownies

Prepare brownies as directed, except stir ½ cup chopped pecans into batter. Sprinkle batter with ½ cup miniature semisweet chocolate pieces. Bake as directed. In a saucepan combine one 6¼-ounce package vanilla caramels and 2 tablespoons milk. Cook and stir over medium-low heat until smooth. Drizzle over brownies. Cool.

Nutrition Facts per Caramel Nut Fudge Brownie: 241 calories, 14 g total fat (4 g saturated fat), 34 mg cholesterol, 91 mg sodium, 28 g carbohydrate, 2 g fiber, 2 g protein.

banana bars

prep: 20 minutes   **bake:** 25 minutes   **oven:** 350°

Toffee, banana, and almond make a sophisticated trio, especially with this buttery frosting. The splash of brandy in the frosting adds just the right accent to these bars.

½ cup butter	½ cup dairy sour cream
1⅓ cups sugar	1 teaspoon vanilla
1½ teaspoons baking powder	2 cups all-purpose flour
½ teaspoon baking soda	¾ cup chocolate-covered toffee pieces or almond brickle pieces
¼ teaspoon salt	¾ cup toasted chopped almonds (optional)
1 egg	1 recipe Brandied Brown Butter Frosting
1 cup mashed bananas (about 3 medium)	

1. Grease a 15x10x1-inch baking pan; set aside.

2. In a large mixing bowl beat the butter with an electric mixer on medium to high speed about 30 seconds. Beat in the sugar, baking powder, baking soda, and salt until combined. Beat in the egg, mashed bananas, sour cream, and vanilla. Beat or stir in the flour. Stir in toffee pieces and, if desired, almonds.

3. Pour the batter into the prepared baking pan, spreading evenly. Bake in a 350° oven about 25 minutes or until a wooden toothpick inserted near the center comes out clean. Cool on a wire rack.

4. Spread with Brandied Brown Butter Frosting. Cut into bars. Makes 48 bars.

Brandied Brown Butter Frosting: In a small saucepan heat ⅓ cup butter over low heat until melted. Continue heating until the butter turns a light brown. Remove from heat; pour into a medium bowl. Add 2½ cups sifted powdered sugar, 1 tablespoon brandy or milk, and 1 teaspoon vanilla. Beat with an electric mixer on low speed until combined. Beat on high to medium speed, adding enough milk to make frosting of spreading consistency. Use immediately.

Nutrition Facts per bar: 115 calories, 5 g total fat (1 g saturated fat), 10 mg cholesterol, 77 mg sodium, 18 g carbohydrate, 0 g fiber, 1 g protein.

mocha brownies

prep: 20 minutes   **bake:** 30 minutes   **oven:** 350°

These buttery mocha brownies boast plenty of semisweet chocolate and a delightful hint of tangerine.

⅔ cup butter
⅓ cup unsweetened cocoa powder
 1 teaspoon instant coffee crystals
 1 cup granulated sugar
 2 eggs
 1 teaspoon vanilla

¾ cup all-purpose flour
½ cup semisweet chocolate pieces or chopped
        semisweet chocolate
 1 teaspoon finely shredded tangerine or
        orange peel
    Powdered sugar (optional)

1. Grease an 8x8x2-inch baking pan; set aside.

2. In a medium saucepan melt the ⅔ cup butter. Stir in the cocoa powder and coffee crystals. Remove from heat. Stir in the granulated sugar. Stir in eggs, 1 at a time, and vanilla. Beat lightly by hand just until combined. Stir in the flour. Stir in the chocolate pieces and the tangerine or orange peel.

3. Spread the batter into the prepared pan. Bake in a 350° oven for 30 minutes. Cool on a wire rack. If desired, sift powdered sugar over top of brownies. Cut into triangles (see below) or bars. Makes 24 brownies.

Nutrition Facts per brownie: 123 calories, 7 g total fat (2 g saturated fat), 24 mg cholesterol, 52 mg sodium, 13 g carbohydrate, 1 g fiber, 1 g protein.

a new cut on bars

Bar cookies don't have to be cut the same old way. For a more special way to serve them, try cutting the bars into triangles or diamonds instead. Here's how:

Triangles: Cut the brownies or bar cookies into squares and halve each square diagonally.

Diamonds: Make straight parallel cuts 1 to 1½ inches apart down the length of the pan. Then make diagonal cuts, about 1 to 1½ inches apart, across the width of the pan, keeping the lines as even as possible. You'll have irregularly shaped pieces at each end of the pan, just right for hovering taste-testers.

citrus-hazelnut bars

prep: 20 minutes   **bake:** 10 minutes/20 minutes   **oven:** 350°

Definitely a bar cookie with lots of appeal—these double citrus and nutty delights are not overly sweet and make a great accompaniment to an afternoon tea break.

⅓ cup butter
¼ cup granulated sugar
1 cup all-purpose flour
⅓ cup finely chopped toasted hazelnuts
  (filberts) or chopped almonds
2 eggs
¾ cup granulated sugar

2 tablespoons all-purpose flour
1 teaspoon finely shredded orange peel
1 teaspoon finely shredded lemon peel
2 tablespoons orange juice
1 tablespoon lemon juice
½ teaspoon baking powder
  Powdered sugar (optional)

1. For the crust, beat the butter in a medium mixing bowl with an electric mixer on medium to high speed for 30 seconds. Add the ¼ cup granulated sugar. Beat until thoroughly combined. Beat in the 1 cup flour and about half of the nuts until mixture is crumbly.

2. Press mixture into the bottom of an ungreased 8x8x2-inch baking pan. Bake bars in a 350° oven for 10 minutes or until lightly browned.

3. Meanwhile, in a mixing bowl stir together the eggs, the ¾ cup granulated sugar, the 2 tablespoons flour, the orange and lemon peels, orange juice, lemon juice, and

baking powder. Beat for 2 minutes at medium speed or until combined. Pour over hot baked layer. Sprinkle with remaining nuts.

4. Bake about 20 minutes more or until light brown around the edges and center is set. Cool on a wire rack. If desired, sift powdered sugar over top. Cut into bars. Store bars, covered, in the refrigerator. Makes 20 bars.

Nutrition Facts per bar: 111 calories, 5 g total fat
(1 g saturated fat), 25 mg cholesterol, 43 mg sodium,
16 g carbohydrate, 0 g fiber, 2 g protein.

orange-glazed brownies

prep: 20 minutes **bake:** 30 minutes **oven:** 350°

Irresistibly orange and wonderfully chocolate is the only way to describe the rich flavor of these glazed brownies.

4 ounces unsweetened chocolate, chopped
½ cup butter
1 cup sugar
2 eggs
2 teaspoons finely shredded orange peel

1 teaspoon vanilla
¾ cup all-purpose flour
½ cup coarsely chopped walnuts or pecans
1 recipe Chocolate-Orange Glaze

1. In a medium saucepan combine the unsweetened chocolate and butter; heat and stir over low heat until melted. Remove from heat. Stir in the sugar, eggs, orange peel, and vanilla. Using a wooden spoon, lightly beat mixture just until combined. Stir in flour and nuts.

2. Spread batter into an ungreased 8x8x2-inch baking pan. Bake in a 350° oven for 30 minutes. Cool on a wire rack.

3. Pour Chocolate-Orange Glaze over the cooled brownies, spreading to glaze the top evenly. Let brownies stand at room temperature until glaze is set. Cut into bars. Makes 9 brownies.

Chocolate-Orange Glaze: In a heavy, small saucepan bring ⅓ cup whipping cream to a gentle boil over medium-low heat, stirring constantly. Remove from heat. Add 3 ounces finely chopped semisweet chocolate and 1 teaspoon finely shredded orange peel. Let stand for 1 minute. Using a wooden spoon, stir mixture until chocolate is melted. Cool glaze for 5 minutes before using.

Nutrition Facts per brownie: 413 calories, 29 g total fat (10 g saturated fat), 73 mg cholesterol, 113 mg sodium, 41 g carbohydrate, 2 g fiber, 6 g protein.

citrus appeal

If a recipe calls for grated or shredded orange, lime, or lemon peel, use only the colored surface of the peel, not the spongy white pith, which tastes bitter.

Hand graters and zesters are convenient, but you can also use a vegetable parer to remove layers of peel. Then, finely mince the peel with a sharp kitchen knife.

Make extra peel to keep on hand. Layer it between paper towels and freeze in a resealable bag.

buttermilk brownies

prep: 30 minutes   **bake:** 25 minutes   **oven:** 350°

Luscious brownies with a cocoa-rich frosting get a little extra zing from the tang of buttermilk. For a spiced brownie, try the cinnamon variation.

 2 cups all-purpose flour
 2 cups sugar
 1 teaspoon baking soda
 ¼ teaspoon salt
 1 cup butter
 1 cup water

 ⅓ cup unsweetened cocoa powder
 2 eggs
 ½ cup buttermilk
 1½ teaspoons vanilla
 1 recipe Chocolate-Buttermilk Frosting

1. Grease a 15x10x1-inch or a 13x9x2-inch baking pan; set aside. In a medium mixing bowl combine the flour, sugar, baking soda, and salt; set aside.

2. In a medium saucepan combine butter, water, and cocoa powder. Bring mixture just to boiling, stirring constantly. Remove from heat. Add the chocolate mixture to the flour mixture; beat with an electric mixer on medium speed until combined. Add the eggs, buttermilk, and vanilla. Beat for 1 minute (batter will be thin). Pour batter into the prepared pan.

3. Bake brownies in a 350° oven about 25 minutes for the 15x10x1-inch pan, 35 minutes for the 13x9x2-inch pan, or until a wooden toothpick inserted in the center comes out clean.

4. Pour warm Chocolate Buttermilk Frosting over the warm brownies, spreading evenly. Cool on a wire rack. Cut into bars. Makes 24 brownies.

Chocolate-Buttermilk Frosting: In a medium saucepan combine ¼ cup butter, 3 tablespoons unsweetened cocoa powder, and 3 tablespoons buttermilk. Bring mixture to boiling. Remove from heat. Add 2¼ cups sifted powdered sugar and ½ teaspoon vanilla. Beat until smooth. If desired, stir in ¾ cup coarsely chopped pecans.

Cinnamon-Buttermilk Brownies: Prepare brownies as directed, except add 1 teaspoon ground cinnamon to the flour mixture.

Nutrition Facts per brownie: 237 calories, 10 g total fat
(6 g saturated fat), 44 mg cholesterol, 185 mg sodium,
35 g carbohydrate, 0 g fiber, 2 g protein.

dandy drop

white-chocolate-raspberry cookies

prep: 30 minutes   **bake:** 7 minutes   **oven:** 375°

If it's your turn to host the Christmas party or the block party, try these festive melt-in-your-mouth cookies. They're elegant and sophisticated enough to serve as a simple dessert.

8   ounces white baking bar
½   cup butter
1   cup sugar
1   teaspoon baking soda
¼   teaspoon salt

2   eggs
2¾   cups all-purpose flour
½   cup seedless raspberry jam
3   ounces white baking bar
½   teaspoon shortening

1. Grease a cookie sheet; set aside. Chop 4 ounces of the white baking bar; set aside. In a heavy small saucepan, melt the 4 ounces of the white baking bar over low heat while stirring constantly; cool.

2. In a large mixing bowl beat butter with an electric mixer on medium to high speed 30 seconds. Add the sugar, baking soda, and salt. Beat until combined. Beat in eggs and melted white baking bar until combined. Beat in as much of the flour as you can with the mixer. Stir in remaining flour. Stir in the 4 ounces of chopped white baking bar.

3. Drop dough by a rounded teaspoon about 2 inches apart onto the prepared cookie sheet. Bake cookies in a 375° oven for 7 to 9 minutes or until edges are lightly browned. Cool on cookie sheet for 1 minute. Transfer to a wire rack; cool.

4. Just before serving, in a small saucepan melt the raspberry jam over low heat. Spoon about ½ teaspoon of jam onto the top of each cookie. In a heavy, small saucepan combine the 3 ounces white baking bar and shortening. Melt over low heat, stirring constantly. Drizzle each cookie with some of the melted mixture. If necessary, refrigerate about 15 minutes to firm baking bar mixture. Makes about 48 cookies.

To make ahead: Bake and cool cookies as directed. Do not decorate. Place in a freezer-proof container; freeze for up to 1 month. Before serving, thaw for 15 minutes. Drizzle as directed.

Nutrition Facts per cookie: 104 calories, 4 g total fat (2 g saturated fat), 14 mg cholesterol, 66 mg sodium, 16 g carbohydrate, 0 g fiber, 1 g protein.

& roll

Many of the all-time-favorite cookies are simple drop or roll cookies.

This selection of dandies will make it hard to choose which to make next.

fall fruit drops

prep: 35 minutes   **bake:** 9 minutes   **oven:** 375°

If you haven't used hickory nuts, give them a try in this fruit-filled cookie. Hickory nuts have a rich, buttery flavor.

⅔ cup golden raisins, snipped dried apricots, and/or
     chopped, pitted dates
⅓ cup apple juice or apple cider
½ cup butter
⅔ cup granulated sugar
⅔ cup packed brown sugar
1½ teaspoons apple pie spice

½ teaspoon baking soda
¼ teaspoon salt
1 egg
2¼ cups all-purpose flour
¾ cup shredded apple
1 recipe Apple-Cream Cheese Frosting
⅔ cup chopped hickory nuts or black walnuts
     (optional)

1. In a bowl stir together the raisins, apricots, or dates, and apple juice or cider. Let stand for 15 minutes. Drain fruit, reserving liquid. Grease a cookie sheet; set aside.

2. In a large mixing bowl beat the butter with an electric mixer on medium to high speed about 30 seconds. Add the granulated sugar, brown sugar, apple pie spice, baking soda, and salt; beat until combined. Beat in the egg and the reserved liquid. Beat in as much of the flour as you can with the mixer. Stir in remaining flour, the shredded apple, the raisin mixture, and, if desired, the chopped hickory nuts or black walnuts.

3. Drop dough by a rounded teaspoon 2 inches apart onto prepared cookie sheet. Bake cookies in a 375° oven for 9 to 11 minutes or until edges are lightly browned. Cool on cookie sheet for 1 minute. Transfer cookies to a wire rack; cool. Frost cookies with Apple-Cream Cheese Frosting. Store cookies in an airtight container in the refrigerator. Makes 48 cookies.

Apple-Cream Cheese Frosting: In a medium mixing bowl combine one 3-ounce package cream cheese, softened; ¼ cup butter, softened; and 1 teaspoon vanilla. Beat with an electric mixer on medium to high speed until fluffy. Gradually beat in 1 cup sifted powdered sugar, beating well. Gradually beat in 1¾ cups additional sifted powdered sugar and enough apple juice or apple cider (about 2 to 3 tablespoons) to make frosting easy to spread.

Nutrition Facts per cookie: 105 calories, 4 g total fat
(2 g saturated fat), 14 mg cholesterol, 61 mg sodium,
18 g carbohydrate, 0 g fiber, 1 g protein.

chocolate-almond sugar cookies

prep: 25 minutes   **bake:** 7 minutes   **oven:** 375°

Your choice of liqueur adds a grown-up flavor to these rich chocolate chip cookies.

4 cups all-purpose flour	3 tablespoons amaretto, coffee liqueur, crème
½ cup unsweetened cocoa powder	de cacao, or milk
⅔ cup shortening	2 teaspoons vanilla
⅔ cup butter	1 cup miniature semisweet chocolate pieces
1½ cups sugar	¾ cup finely chopped almonds or pecans
2 teaspoons baking powder	Sugar
2 eggs	

1. In a medium mixing bowl stir together the flour and cocoa powder; set aside.

2. In a large mixing bowl beat shortening and butter with an electric mixer on medium to high speed for 30 seconds. Add the sugar and baking powder; beat until combined. Beat in eggs, liqueur or milk, and vanilla until combined. Beat in as much of the flour mixture as you can with the mixer. Stir in remaining flour mixture. Stir in chocolate pieces and nuts.

3. Drop dough by a rounded teaspoon 2 inches apart onto an ungreased cookie sheet. Flatten each piece of dough with a glass dipped in sugar. Bake cookies in a 375° oven for 7 to 9 minutes or until edges are firm. Transfer cookies to a wire rack; cool. Makes about 72 cookies.

Nutrition Facts per cookie: 100 calories, 5 g total fat (1 g saturated fat), 8 mg cholesterol, 28 mg sodium, 11 g carbohydrate, 1 g fiber, 1 g protein.

cashew meringues

prep: 25 minutes   **bake:** 15 minutes   **oven:** 325°

A drizzling of caramel and a sprinkling of cashews make these melt-in-your-mouth cookies irresistible.

4 egg whites
1 teaspoon vanilla
¼ teaspoon cream of tartar
4 cups sifted powdered sugar

2 cups chopped cashews or mixed nuts
12 vanilla caramels, unwrapped
2 teaspoons milk

1. In a large mixing bowl allow egg whites to stand at room temperature for 30 minutes. Meanwhile, grease a cookie sheet; set aside.

2. Add vanilla and cream of tartar to egg whites. Beat with an electric mixer on medium speed until soft peaks form (tips curl). Gradually add the powdered sugar, about ¼ cup at a time, beating on medium speed just until combined. Beat for 1 to 2 minutes more or until soft peaks form. (Do not continue beating to stiff peaks.) Using a spoon, gently fold in the cashews or mixed nuts.

3. Drop egg white mixture by a rounded teaspoon about 2 inches apart onto prepared cookie sheet. Bake cookies in a 325° oven about 15 minutes or until edges are very lightly browned. Transfer cookies to a wire rack; cool.

4. In a small saucepan combine the caramels and milk. Heat and stir over low heat until the caramels are melted. Place cookies on a wire rack over waxed paper. Drizzle caramel mixture over cookies. If desired, sprinkle with additional chopped cashews or mixed nuts. Let stand until caramel mixture is set. Makes 60 cookies.

Nutrition Facts per cookie: 61 calories, 2 g total fat (1 g saturated fat), 0 mg cholesterol, 9 mg sodium, 10 g carbohydrate, 0 g fiber, 1 g protein.

frosted sour cream-chocolate drops

prep: 30 minutes   **bake:** 8 minutes   **oven:** 350°

These deep chocolate delights—topped with a chocolate-butter cream frosting—are just too tempting. So that they don't disappear all at once, you might want to store some out of sight.

½ cup butter
1 cup packed brown sugar
½ teaspoon baking soda
¼ teaspoon salt
1 8-ounce carton dairy sour cream

2 ounces unsweetened chocolate, melted
   and cooled
1 egg
1 teaspoon vanilla
2 cups all-purpose flour
1 recipe Chocolate Butter Frosting

1. In a large mixing bowl beat butter with an electric mixer on medium to high speed for 30 seconds. Add the brown sugar, baking soda, and salt. Beat until combined, scraping sides of bowl occasionally. Beat in the sour cream, melted chocolate, egg, and vanilla until combined. Beat in as much of the flour as you can with the mixer. Stir in remaining flour.

2. Drop dough by a slightly rounded teaspoon about 3 inches apart onto an ungreased cookie sheet. Bake cookies in a 350° oven for 8 to 10 minutes or until edges are firm. Transfer cookies to a wire rack; cool.

3. Spread cooled cookies with Chocolate Butter Frosting. Makes 42 cookies.

Chocolate Butter Frosting: In a medium mixing bowl beat ¼ cup butter until fluffy. Gradually add 1 cup sifted powdered sugar and ⅓ cup unsweetened cocoa powder, beating well. Slowly beat in 3 tablespoons milk and 1 teaspoon vanilla. Slowly beat in an additional 1½ cups sifted powdered sugar. If necessary, beat in additional milk to make frosting of spreading consistency.

Nutrition Facts per cookie: 111 calories, 5 g total fat (3 g saturated fat), 16 mg cholesterol, 67 mg sodium, 15 g carbohydrate, 0 g fiber, 1 g protein.

drop it right

Drop cookies are some of the easiest cookies to make, but there are a few tricks:

- Use a spoon from your daily flatware—not a measuring spoon—to drop them. The deeper bowl of measuring spoons makes the dough harder to remove.
- Keep dough mounds the same size. Space dough evenly on the cookie sheet; don't crowd cookies.
- Use only a light coating of shortening if the recipe calls for a greased pan. Too much will cause the cookies to spread and flatten.
- Don't drop cookie dough onto a hot cookie sheet. Use two sheets or cool the sheet between batches.

fruit-and-nut oatmeal cookies

prep: 30 minutes   **bake:** 8 minutes   **oven:** 375°

These are not ordinary oatmeal cookies. Dried cranberries complement the orange flavor which abounds in both the cookie and the icing.

½ cup shortening
½ cup butter
1 cup granulated sugar
1 cup packed brown sugar
2 teaspoons finely shredded orange peel
1 teaspoon ground cinnamon
½ teaspoon baking soda
½ teaspoon salt
2 eggs

2 tablespoons orange juice
3 cups all-purpose flour
1¾ cups quick-cooking rolled oats
⅔ cup finely chopped dried cranberries,
     dried tart cherries, or dried currants
½ cup finely chopped hazelnuts (filberts) or
     walnuts
1 recipe Orange Icing (optional)

1. In a large mixing bowl beat shortening and butter with an electric mixer on medium to high speed for 30 seconds. Add the granulated sugar, brown sugar, orange peel, cinnamon, baking soda, and salt; beat until combined. Beat in the eggs and orange juice. Beat in as much of the flour as you can with a mixer. Stir in remaining flour, the rolled oats, fruit, and nuts.

2. Drop dough by a rounded teaspoon about 2 inches apart onto an ungreased cookie sheet. Bake cookies in a 375° oven about 8 minutes or until edges are lightly browned. Cool on cookie sheet for 1 minute. Transfer cookies to a wire rack; cool.

3. To glaze, place cookies on a wire rack over waxed paper. Drizzle Orange Icing over cookies. Let icing dry. Makes 54 cookies.

Orange Icing: In a small mixing bowl stir together 2 cups sifted powdered sugar and enough orange juice (2 to 3 tablespoons) to make drizzling consistency.

Nutrition Facts per cookie: 108 calories, 5 g total fat (2 g saturated fat), 12 mg cholesterol, 63 mg sodium, 15 g carbohydrate, 1 g fiber, 1 g protein.

chocolate-covered cherry cookies

prep: 30 minutes   **bake:** 10 minutes   **oven:** 350°

What a neat trick: These cookies are frosted before they're baked! Under the frosting hides a plump, red cherry.

1½ cups all-purpose flour
½ cup unsweetened cocoa powder
48 undrained maraschino cherries (about
      one 10-ounce jar)
½ cup butter
1 cup sugar
¼ teaspoon baking soda

¼ teaspoon baking powder
¼ teaspoon salt
1 egg
1½ teaspoons vanilla
1 6-ounce package semisweet chocolate pieces
½ cup sweetened condensed milk

1. Combine the flour and cocoa powder; set aside. Drain the maraschino cherries, reserving juice. Place cherries on paper towels to drain thoroughly; set aside.

2. In a mixing bowl beat butter with an electric mixer until softened. Add the sugar, soda, baking powder, and salt. Beat until combined. Add the egg and vanilla; beat to combine. Gradually beat in the flour mixture.

3. Shape dough into 1-inch balls; place on an ungreased cookie sheet. Press down center of each ball with your thumb. Place one cherry in the center of each cookie.

4. For frosting, in a small saucepan combine the chocolate pieces and sweetened condensed milk; heat until chocolate is melted. Stir in 4 teaspoons of the reserved cherry juice.

5. Spoon about 1 teaspoon of frosting over each cherry, spreading to cover cherry. If necessary, thin frosting with additional cherry juice. Bake cookies in a 350° oven about 10 minutes or until edges are firm. Remove to a wire rack; cool. Makes 48 cookies.

Nutrition Facts per cookie: 81 calories, 3 g total fat
(1 g saturated fat), 11 mg cholesterol, 45 mg sodium,
12 g carbohydrate, 0 g fiber, 1 g protein.

oatmeal jumbos

prep: 35 minutes   **bake:** 15 minutes   **oven:** 350°

Make these cookies large or small. Both sizes are big in peanut butter and chocolate taste.

1 cup peanut butter	3 eggs
½ cup butter	2 teaspoons vanilla
1½ cups packed brown sugar	4 cups rolled oats
½ cup granulated sugar	¾ cup chopped peanuts, walnuts, or pecans
1½ teaspoons baking powder	1½ cups candy-coated milk chocolate pieces
½ teaspoon baking soda	

1. In a large mixing bowl beat the peanut butter and butter with an electric mixer on medium to high speed for 30 seconds. Add the brown sugar, granulated sugar, baking powder, and baking soda; beat until combined. Beat in the eggs and vanilla until combined. Stir in the rolled oats. Stir in the nuts and the candy-coated milk chocolate pieces.

2. Drop dough by a ¼-cup measure or scoop 4 inches apart onto an ungreased cookie sheet. Bake cookies in a 350° oven about 15 minutes or until edges are lightly browned. (Or, for small cookies, drop dough by a rounded teaspoon about 2 inches apart onto an ungreased cookie sheet. Bake cookies in a 350° oven about 10 minutes or until edges are lightly browned.) Cool 1 minute on the cookie sheet.

3. Transfer cookies to a wire rack; cool. Makes 26 large or about 60 small cookies.

Nutrition Facts per large cookie: 272 calories, 14 g total fat (4 g saturated fat), 34 mg cholesterol, 173 mg sodium, 32 g carbohydrate, 2 g fiber, 7 g protein.

fudge ecstasies

prep: 20 minutes   **bake:** 8 minutes   **oven:** 350°

You'll think you broke the chocolate bank when you bite into one of these chewy, double-chocolate, nut-filled wonders.

1 12-ounce package (2 cups) semisweet chocolate pieces	⅔ cup sugar
2 ounces unsweetened chocolate, chopped	¼ cup all-purpose flour
2 tablespoons butter	1 teaspoon vanilla
2 eggs	¼ teaspoon baking powder
	1 cup chopped nuts

1. Grease a cookie sheet; set aside. In a heavy, medium saucepan combine 1 cup of the chocolate pieces, the unsweetened chocolate, and butter; heat and stir over medium-low heat until melted. Remove from heat. Add the eggs, sugar, flour, vanilla, and baking powder. Beat until combined, scraping sides of pan occasionally. Stir in remaining chocolate pieces and nuts.

2. Drop dough by a rounded teaspoon about 2 inches apart onto the prepared cookie sheet. Bake cookies in a 350° oven for 8 to 10 minutes or until edges are firm and surfaces are dull and slightly cracked. Transfer the cookies to a wire rack; cool. Makes about 36 cookies.

Nutrition Facts per cookie: 101 calories, 6 g total fat (1 g saturated fat), 14 mg cholesterol, 13 mg sodium, 12 g carbohydrate, 0 g fiber, 2 g protein.

chocolate sense

When a recipe calls for chocolate, the higher the quality of the chocolate you use, the better the results. Chocolate is a combination of cocoa butter, chocolate "liquor" (the pressed liquid from roasted cocoa beans), and sugar. An imitation chocolate may substitute vegetable fat for the cocoa butter.

Some recipes call for white chocolate. Although not truly chocolate, since it contains none of the chocolate liquor from the cocoa bean, white chocolate should contain cocoa butter. Use only a high-quality white chocolate when baking.

orange-macadamia nut cookies

prep: 35 minutes   **bake:** 12 minutes   **oven:** 350°

Buttery tasting macadamia nuts give these cookies a wonderful flavor. The rich flavor is most likely due to the nuts' high fat content. So they don't turn rancid, store any extra nuts in an airtight container in the refrigerator or freezer.

4 cups all-purpose flour
2 cups sifted powdered sugar
1 cup cornstarch
2 cups butter
1 cup chopped macadamia nuts or toasted walnuts
2 beaten egg yolks

1 tablespoon finely shredded orange peel
4 to 6 tablespoons orange juice
   Granulated sugar
1 recipe Orange Frosting
   Finely shredded orange peel (optional)

1. In a large mixing bowl stir together flour, powdered sugar, and cornstarch. Using a pastry blender, cut in butter until mixture resembles coarse crumbs. Stir in nuts. In a small mixing bowl combine egg yolks, the 1 tablespoon orange peel, and 4 tablespoons of the orange juice; add to flour mixture, stirring until moistened. If necessary, add enough of the remaining orange juice to moisten.

2. Knead dough on a lightly floured surface until it forms a ball. Shape dough into 1¼-inch balls. Place balls about 2 inches apart on an ungreased cookie sheet. Using the bottom of a glass dipped in granulated sugar, flatten dough to ¼-inch thickness.

3. Bake cookies in a 350° oven for 12 to 15 minutes or until edges begin to brown. Transfer cookies to a wire rack; cool. Spread cooled cookies with Orange Frosting. If desired, garnish with finely shredded orange peel. Makes 72 cookies.

Orange Frosting: Stir together 2 cups sifted powdered sugar, 3 tablespoons softened butter, 1 teaspoon finely shredded orange peel, and enough orange juice (2 to 3 tablespoons) to make of spreading consistency.

Nutrition Facts per cookie: 120 calories, 7 g total fat (2 g saturated fat), 13 mg cholesterol, 56 mg sodium, 13 g carbohydrate, 0 g fiber, 1 g protein.

peanut-packed praline cookies

prep: 35 minutes   **bake:** 8 minutes   **chill:** 1 to 2 hours   **oven:** 375°

Southern or not, almost everyone will love these peanutty cookies. Bring a batch of these home-style Southern goodies to your next family reunion.

½ cup shortening
½ cup peanut butter
½ cup granulated sugar
½ cup packed brown sugar
1 teaspoon baking soda
1 egg

2 tablespoons milk
1 teaspoon vanilla
1¼ cups all-purpose flour
1½ cups coarsely chopped peanuts
1 recipe Praline Frosting

1. In a large mixing bowl beat the shortening and peanut butter with an electric mixer on medium speed for 30 seconds. Add the granulated sugar, brown sugar, and baking soda. Beat until combined, scraping sides of bowl. Beat in egg, milk, and vanilla until combined. Beat in as much of the flour as you can with the mixer. Stir in remaining flour. Stir in peanuts. If necessary, cover and chill in the refrigerator for 1 to 2 hours or until dough is easy to handle.

2. Shape dough into 1¼-inch balls. Place balls 2 inches apart on an ungreased cookie sheet. Bake cookies in a 375° oven for 8 to 10 minutes or until edges are firm. Transfer cookies to a wire rack; cool. Drizzle cooled cookies with Praline Frosting. Makes 48 cookies.

Praline Frosting: In a small saucepan combine ½ cup packed brown sugar and ¼ cup whipping cream. Cook and stir until bubbly. Reduce heat and simmer for 2 minutes. Remove pan from heat. Beat in 1 cup sifted powdered sugar until smooth. If necessary, add enough hot water, 1 teaspoon at a time, to make of drizzling consistency. Immediately drizzle onto cooled cookies.

Nutrition Facts per cookie: 109 calories, 6 g total fat
(1 g saturated fat), 6 mg cholesterol, 79 mg sodium,
12 g carbohydrate, 1 g fiber, 2 g protein.

chilling out

Many cookie recipes call for chilling the dough in the refrigerator before shaping or cutting. This helps to stiffen the butter or shortening and make the dough more manageable. It also makes the finished product better, since chilled dough needs to be worked less than an unchilled dough.

lemon-poppy seed cookies

prep: 25 minutes   **bake:** 8 minutes   **chill:** 1 hour   **oven:** 375°

Your mom might remember these cookies from when she was a little girl. Lemon and poppy seed butter cookies were already a time-honored classic by the 1930s.

1 cup butter
1 cup granulated sugar
1 egg
1 teaspoon vanilla
2 teaspoons poppy seed

1 teaspoon finely shredded lemon peel
2 cups all-purpose flour
   Granulated sugar
   Powdered sugar (optional)

1. In a large mixing bowl beat the butter with an electric mixer on medium to high speed for 30 seconds. Add the 1 cup sugar. Beat until combined. Beat in the egg and vanilla. Beat until combined. Beat in poppy seed, lemon peel, and as much of the flour as you can with the mixer. Stir in remaining flour. Cover and chill in the refrigerator for 1 to 2 hours or until easy to handle.

2. Shape dough into 1-inch balls. Place about 2 inches apart on an ungreased cookie sheet. Using the bottom of a glass dipped in additional sugar, slightly flatten balls to ½-inch thickness.

3. Bake cookies in a 375° oven for 8 to 10 minutes or until edges are firm and bottoms are lightly browned. Cool on cookie sheet for 1 minute. Transfer cookies to a wire rack; cool. If desired, sift powdered sugar over cookies. Makes about 50 cookies.

To make ahead: Bake and cool cookies as directed. Place in layers separated by waxed paper in a freezer container or freezer bag and freeze for up to 1 month. Before serving, thaw for 15 minutes.

Nutrition Facts per cookie: 67 calories, 4 g total fat (2 g saturated fat), 14 mg cholesterol, 39 mg sodium, 8 g carbohydrate, 0 g fiber, 1 g protein.

Using cookie cutters or just a knife to create new shapes from cookie dough is fun. But it's also an art form. Check out these artsy edibles.

cool

tropical pinwheels

prep: 30 minutes   **chill:** 2 hours   **bake:** 8 minutes   **oven:** 350°

Set the wheels in motion for tropical taste with these cookie cutouts. They're bursting with pineapple, coconut, and buttery macadamia nuts.

⅓ cup shortening
⅓ cup butter
¾ cup sugar
1½ teaspoons baking powder
¼ teaspoon salt
1 egg
4 teaspoons milk
1 teaspoon vanilla

2 cups all-purpose flour
1 3-ounce package cream cheese, softened
2 tablespoons sugar
¼ cup coconut
¼ cup finely chopped macadamia nuts or
    almonds
    Colored sugar (optional)
1 recipe Pineapple Icing (optional)

1. In a large mixing bowl beat shortening and butter with an electric mixer on medium to high speed for 30 seconds. Add the ¾ cup sugar, the baking powder, and salt; beat until combined. Beat in egg, milk, and vanilla, scraping sides of the bowl occasionally. Beat in as much of the flour as you can with the mixer. Stir in remaining flour. Divide dough in half. Cover and chill in the refrigerator about 3 hours or until dough is easy to handle.

2. For filling, in a small bowl stir together softened cream cheese and the 2 tablespoons sugar. Stir in the coconut.

3. On a lightly floured surface, roll half of dough into a 10-inch square. Using a fluted pastry wheel or a sharp knife, cut square into sixteen 2½-inch squares. Place squares 2 inches apart on an ungreased cookie sheet. Cut 1-inch slits from each corner toward the center of each square. Spoon a level teaspoon of the filling in each center. Fold every other tip to center to form a pinwheel,

pressing lightly to seal the tips. Carefully sprinkle some of the chopped nuts onto the center of each pinwheel; press nuts lightly into the dough. If desired, sprinkle cookies with colored sugar.

4. Bake cookies in a 350° oven for 8 to 10 minutes or until the edges are lightly browned. Cool for 1 minute. Transfer cookies to a wire rack; cool. Repeat with remaining dough and filling. If desired, drizzle with Pineapple Icing and sprinkle with additional colored sugar. Makes 32 cookies.

Pineapple Icing: In a small bowl stir together ¾ cup sifted powdered sugar and enough pineapple juice (about 1 tablespoon) to make icing of drizzling consistency.

Nutrition Facts per cookie: 105 calories, 6 g total fat
(3 g saturated fat), 15 mg cholesterol, 63 mg sodium,
12 g carbohydrate, 0 g fiber, 1 g protein.

cutouts

orange spice houses

prep: 30 minutes **bake:** 8 minutes **oven:** 375°

Let everyone create a holiday dream house. Here's a recipe for some sweet structures that are prefab fabulous.

1½ cups butter
2 cups packed brown sugar
1 teaspoon baking powder
1 teaspoon ground cinnamon
1 teaspoon finely shredded orange peel
½ teaspoon salt
½ teaspoon ground ginger
¼ teaspoon ground cloves
1 beaten egg
3½ cups all-purpose flour
  Purchased decorator icing (optional)
  Candies for decorating, such as colored hard
    candies; tiny mints; mini jelly beans, halved;
    gumdrops; and broken candy canes (optional)

1. In a medium mixing bowl beat butter with an electric mixer on medium to high speed for 30 seconds. Add the brown sugar, baking powder, cinnamon, orange peel, salt, ginger, and cloves; beat until fluffy. Beat in the egg. Gradually beat in as much of the flour as you can with the mixer. Stir in remaining flour. (Dough will be stiff.) Divide dough into thirds.

2. On a well-floured pastry cloth, roll one-third of the dough to ¼-inch thickness. Place a house or barn pattern* on the dough. Cut around the pattern using a small sharp knife. (Or, if desired, cut dough using a 3- to 4-inch house-shaped cookie cutter.) With a floured metal spatula, transfer the cookies to ungreased cookie sheets, placing the cookies about 2½ inches apart.

3. Bake cookies in a 375° oven about 8 minutes or until edges are lightly browned. Transfer cookies to a wire rack; cool. Repeat with remaining dough.

4. Decorate cookies as desired with decorator icing and assorted candies. Makes about 60 cookies.

Nutrition Facts per cookie: 93 calories, 5 g total fat
(3 g saturated fat), 16 mg cholesterol, 68 mg sodium,
12 g carbohydrate, 0 g fiber, 1 g protein.

*__Note:__ To make your own house or barn pattern, use poster board or sturdy paper. The height from the rooftop to floor should be about 3 inches and the width about 2½ inches.

blossom cookies

prep: 25 minutes   **chill:** 2 hours   **bake:** 6 minutes   **oven:** 375°

Four heart-shaped pieces of dough, positioned just right, blend during baking to create a flower-shaped cookie.

¼ cup butter
½ cup sugar
1 egg
1 tablespoon milk
½ teaspoon vanilla

1¼ cups self-rising flour
1 recipe Powdered Sugar Icing
    Miniature candy-coated milk
        chocolate pieces

1. Lightly grease a cookie sheet; set aside. In a medium mixing bowl beat butter with an electric mixer on medium speed for 30 seconds. Add sugar and beat until combined. Beat in egg, milk, and vanilla. Stir in flour. Divide dough in half. Cover and chill dough in refrigerator for 2 hours or until easy to handle.

2. On a lightly floured surface, roll half of the dough to ⅛ inch thickness. Cut with a 1-inch heart-shaped cookie cutter. For each cookie, arrange 4 hearts on prepared cookie sheet, points together and 1 or 2 of the sides overlapping slightly. Repeat with remaining dough.

3. Bake cookies in a 375° oven for 6 to 7 minutes or until the edges are slightly golden brown. Cool on cookie sheet for 1 minute. Transfer to a wire rack.

4. Using a large pastry brush, brush the warm cookies with Powdered Sugar Icing. Place a candy-coated chocolate piece in the center of each cookie. Let cookies stand until icing is set. Makes about 60 cookies.

Powdered Sugar Icing: Stir together 1 cup sifted strawberry- or lemon-flavored powdered sugar, ¼ teaspoon vanilla, and 1 tablespoon milk. Stir in enough additional milk, 1 teaspoon at a time, to make icing of drizzling consistency.

Nutrition Facts per cookie: 45 calories, 2 g total fat
(0 g saturated fat), 5 mg cholesterol, 44 mg sodium,
7 g carbohydrate, 0 g fiber, 1 g protein.

cornmeal diamonds

prep: 50 minutes   **chill:** 3 hours   **bake:** 7 minutes   **oven:** 375°

Hold an art contest. Give each of your kids a fine-tipped brush and food coloring, so they can paint the glazed cookies.
For inexpensive brushes, purchase small eyeliner makeup brushes (look in your supermarket's makeup section).

⅔ cup butter	1 teaspoon vanilla
⅔ cup sugar	½ cup yellow cornmeal
1 teaspoon baking powder	1½ cups all-purpose flour
¼ teaspoon salt	1 recipe Lemon Glaze (optional)
1 egg	Food coloring (optional)
1½ teaspoons finely shredded lemon peel	

1. In a large bowl beat butter with an electric mixer on medium to high speed for 30 seconds. Add sugar, baking powder, and salt; beat until combined. Beat in egg, lemon peel, and vanilla. Beat in cornmeal and as much of the flour as you can with the mixer. Stir in remaining flour.

2. Divide dough in half. Wrap each half in waxed paper or plastic wrap and chill in refrigerator for 3 hours, or until dough is easy to handle.

3. On a lightly floured surface, roll half of dough to slightly less than ¼-inch thickness. Using a 2-inch-long scalloped diamond cookie cutter, cut dough. Place diamonds 1 inch apart on an ungreased cookie sheet.

4. Bake cookies in a 375° oven for 7 to 8 minutes or until edges are lightly browned. Transfer the cookies to a wire rack; cool. Repeat with remaining dough. If desired, frost cookies with Lemon Glaze. Let glaze dry before serving. If desired, using a small fine-tipped brush and food coloring, paint designs on the cookies (see photos, *opposite page*). Makes about 54 cookies.

Lemon Glaze: In a small mixing bowl stir together 1½ cups sifted powdered sugar, 2 teaspoons lemon juice, and enough milk (1 to 2 tablespoons) to make of spreading consistency.

Cornmeal-Cherry Diamonds: Prepare cookies as directed, except stir ⅓ cup finely snipped dried tart cherries in with the flour and cornmeal.

Nutrition Facts per cookie: 58 calories,
2 g total fat (1 g saturated fat),
10 mg cholesterol, 41 mg sodium,
9 g carbohydrate, 0 g fiber, 1 g protein.

sesame pecan wafers

prep: 30 minutes   **chill:** 1 hour   **bake:** 7 minutes   **oven:** 375°

Serve these nutty, Southern-style wafers as a complement to a generous scoop of your favorite ice cream.

1 cup butter
⅔ cup sugar
1 teaspoon vanilla
1¾ cups all-purpose flour

½ cup sesame seed
½ cup ground pecans or almonds
2 ounces semisweet chocolate
½ teaspoon shortening

1. In a large mixing bowl beat butter with an electric mixer on medium to high speed for 30 seconds. Add the sugar and vanilla; beat until combined. Beat in as much of the flour as you can with the mixer. Stir in remaining flour, the sesame seed, and the pecans or almonds. Divide dough in half. If dough is too sticky to handle, wrap each half in waxed paper or plastic wrap and chill in the refrigerator about 1 hour or until dough is easy to handle.

2. On a lightly floured surface, roll half of the dough to ⅛-inch thickness. Using 2-inch cookie cutters, cut dough into desired shapes. Place 1 inch apart on an ungreased cookie sheet.

3. Bake cookies in a 375° oven for 7 to 8 minutes or until edges are lightly browned. Transfer cookies to a wire rack; cool. Repeat with remaining dough.

4. In a heavy, small saucepan combine semisweet chocolate and shortening; heat over low heat until melted, stirring occasionally. Drizzle chocolate mixture over cookies. Let cookies stand until chocolate is set. Makes 56 cookies.

Nutrition Facts per cookie: 70 calories, 5 g total fat (2 g saturated fat), 9 mg cholesterol, 34 mg sodium, 6 g carbohydrate, 0 g fiber, 1 g protein.

chocolate pistachio hearts

prep: 40 minutes   **bake:** 8 minutes   **oven:** 375°

Pistachios inside and out make this romantic Valentine cookie one to remember. Layer cookies and tissue paper in a pretty box and give them to your sweetheart.

¾ cup butter
¾ cup sugar
½ teaspoon baking powder
1 beaten egg
½ teaspoon vanilla
2 ounces unsweetened chocolate,
   melted and cooled
1¾ cups all-purpose flour

½ cup finely chopped pistachio nuts,
   hazelnuts, or almonds
¾ cup semisweet chocolate pieces
1 tablespoon shortening
¼ cup ground pistachio nuts, hazelnuts,
   or almonds

1. In a large mixing bowl beat butter with an electric mixer on medium to high speed for 30 seconds. Beat in the sugar and baking powder until combined. Beat in the egg and vanilla until well combined. Beat in the melted chocolate. Gradually beat or stir flour into the chocolate mixture. Stir in the ½ cup finely chopped pistachio nuts, hazelnuts, or almonds. Divide dough in half. Cover and, if necessary, chill in the refrigerator until easy to handle.

2. On a lightly floured surface, roll half of dough to ¼-inch thickness. Using a 2-inch heart-shaped cookie cutter, cut into hearts. Place cookies about 2 inches apart on an ungreased cookie sheet.

3. Bake cookies in a 375° oven about 8 minutes or until firm. Transfer cookies to a wire rack; cool.

4. In a heavy, small saucepan combine the chocolate pieces and shortening; heat and stir over medium-low heat until melted. Dip half of each heart into the chocolate mixture. Sprinkle the chocolate with the ¼ cup ground pistachio nuts, hazelnuts, or almonds. Place on wire racks; let stand until chocolate is set. Makes 40 cookies.

Nutrition Facts per cookie: 103 calories, 7 g total fat
(3 g saturated fat), 15 mg cholesterol, 44 mg sodium,
11 g carbohydrate, 0 g fiber, 2 g protein.

joe froggers

prep: 30 minutes   **chill:** 3 hours   **bake:** 9 minutes   **oven:** 375°

Whether so-named because they were as big as the lily pads on Uncle Joe's pond—or from a corruption of "grogger," slang for a rum drinker—the origins of this spice cookie's name are lost in time. Lucky for us the recipe wasn't.

¾ cup butter
1 cup sugar
1½ teaspoons ground ginger
1 teaspoon baking soda
½ teaspoon ground cloves
½ teaspoon ground nutmeg

¼ teaspoon ground allspice
1 cup molasses
2 tablespoons water
2 tablespoons rum or milk
4 cups all-purpose flour

1. Grease a cookie sheet; set aside. In a large mixing bowl beat butter with an electric mixer on medium to high speed for 30 seconds. Add the sugar, ginger, baking soda, cloves, nutmeg, and allspice. Beat until combined. Beat in the molasses, water, and rum or milk until combined. Beat in as much of the flour as you can with the mixer. Stir in remaining flour. Divide dough in half. Cover and chill in the refrigerator for at least 3 hours.

2. On a lightly floured surface, roll half of the dough to about ¼-inch thickness. Using a floured 4-inch-round cookie cutter, cut dough into circles. Place on the prepared cookie sheet.

3. Bake cookies in a 375° oven for 9 to 11 minutes or until edges are firm and bottoms are just lightly browned. Cool on cookie sheet for 1 minute. Transfer cookies to a wire rack; cool. Repeat with remaining dough. Makes about 24 cookies.

Nutrition Facts per cookie: 199 calories, 6 g total fat (1 g saturated fat), 31 mg cholesterol, 88 mg sodium, 0 g carbohydrate, 0 g fiber, 2 g protein.

roll on

You'll most likely have dough scraps left over after you have cut out your cookies. Combine the scraps, handling the dough as little as possible to keep it tender, and reroll the dough on a very lightly floured surface. Using a pastry stocking and cloth will also help prevent the dough from sticking to the surface.

kid-friendly

crispy cereal treats

total prep: 20 minutes   **cook:** 7 minutes

Four ingredients, no baking. The crispy, quintessential after-school treat from your childhood gets a makeover.

Nonstick spray coating
3 tablespoons butter
1 10½-ounce package (about 6 cups) tiny
   marshmallows

6 cups fruit-flavored crisp rice cereal
6 ounces chocolate-flavored or vanilla-flavored
   candy coating, chopped (optional)

1. Line a 13x9x2-inch baking pan with foil, extending the foil over edges of pan. Spray foil with nonstick coating. Set pan aside.

2. In a large saucepan melt butter; add marshmallows. Cook and stir over low heat until marshmallows melt and mixture is smooth. Remove from heat; stir in cereal. With the back of a buttered spoon, press cereal mixture into prepared pan. Cool

3. Use foil to lift cereal mixture out of pan. Using a 2½-inch cookie cutter, cut into desired shapes. (Or, cut into serving-sized pieces using a knife.)

4. If desired, in a small saucepan heat and stir the candy coating over low heat until melted. Dip one-third of each cookie into the melted candy coating and place on waxed paper. Let cookies stand until the coating is firm. Makes about 16 cookies.

Nutrition Facts per cookie: 120 calories, 2 g total fat (1 g saturated fat), 6 mg cholesterol, 110 mg sodium, 25 g carbohydrate, 0 g fiber, 1 g protein.

no bakes

Your kids will have fun helping make these cookies—and learn how to cook in the process. Choose from several rangetop cookies that take 30 minutes or less to fix.

milk chocolate and caramel clusters

total prep: 20 minutes

These sticky, chewy, crunchy, nutty, chocolaty caramel clusters will become a lunch-box favorite.

12 vanilla caramels, unwrapped
½ cup milk chocolate pieces
2 tablespoons water

2 cups honey graham cereal, slightly crushed
    (about 1½ cups)
¾ cup peanuts

1. Line cookie sheets with waxed paper; set aside. In a heavy, medium saucepan combine the caramels, milk chocolate pieces, and water. Heat and stir over low heat until caramels are melted. Remove saucepan from heat. Stir in the cereal and peanuts.

2. Working quickly, drop the mixture from a teaspoon onto waxed paper. Let stand until firm. Makes about 28 cookies.

Nutrition Facts per cookie: 63 calories, 3 g total fat
(1 g saturated fat), 1 mg cholesterol, 56 mg sodium,
8 g carbohydrate, 0 g fiber, 2 g protein.

melting chocolate

Melting chocolate requires a little patience and extra care. If using chocolate squares, coarsely chop the chocolate before melting. If melting over direct heat, put the chocolate in a heavy-bottomed saucepan over the lowest heat. Using a wooden spoon, stir constantly until the chocolate just begins to melt. Remove the saucepan from the heat and continue stirring until smooth. If necessary, return to heat for only a few seconds.

    If you use a microwave, cook the chopped chocolate, uncovered, only until soft. Stir it often to keep the heat evenly distributed through the chocolate.

peanut butter crunch bars

total prep: 25 minutes   **stand:** 1 hour

Peanuts, peanut butter, chocolate, and crispy rice cereal—all the makings of a cookie your kids will find irresistible.

  5 cups crisp rice cereal
  ¾ cup coarsely chopped peanuts
  1 cup light-colored corn syrup

  ½ cup sugar
  1½ cups chunky peanut butter
  ½ cup semisweet chocolate pieces

1. Line a 13x9x2-inch baking pan with foil, extending foil over the edges of pan. In a large mixing bowl combine cereal and peanuts. In a small saucepan combine the syrup and sugar. Cook and stir over medium heat until mixture just boils. Remove saucepan from heat. Stir in the peanut butter until combined.

2. Pour peanut butter mixture over cereal mixture; stir to mix well. Fold in chocolate pieces. Press mixture into prepared pan. Let stand for 1 hour. Lift foil from pan. Cut into bars. Makes 36 bars.

Nutrition Facts per bar: 145 calories, 8 g total fat (2 g saturated fat), 0 mg cholesterol, 119 mg sodium, 17 g carbohydrate, 1 g fiber, 4 g protein.

fruit-nut bites

total prep: 30 minutes   **cool:** 30 minutes

Filled with fruit and crispy cereal, these nutty treats will be a favorite for kids of all ages. If you like, try snipped dried currants or light raisins in place of the mixed dried fruit bits.

⅔ cup light-colored corn syrup
¼ cup butter
1 tablespoon frozen orange juice concentrate, thawed
1 6-ounce package (1¼ cups) mixed dried fruit bits

1 cup chopped toasted pecans or almonds
2 cups crisp sweetened oat cereal flakes with apples and cinnamon, slightly crushed

1. In a medium saucepan combine the corn syrup, butter, and orange juice concentrate. Bring mixture to boiling and boil for 4 minutes. Remove saucepan from heat.

2. Stir in the fruit bits, pecans or almonds, and cereal. Cool. Shape into balls, using 1 rounded teaspoon of mixture for each. Let stand until firm. Makes 36 cookies.

Nutrition Facts per cookie: 69 calories, 3 g total fat (1 g saturated fat), 3 mg cholesterol, 30 mg sodium, 10 g carbohydrate, 0 g fiber, 1 g protein.

toasty nuts

Toasting heightens the flavor of nuts, and it's simple to do. Spread the nuts in a single layer in a shallow baking pan. Bake in a 350° oven for 5 to 10 minutes or until light golden brown, watching carefully and stirring once or twice so nuts don't burn.

Nuts can also be "toasted" in the microwave. Place nuts in a 2-cup measure. Cook, uncovered, on 100 percent power (high) until light golden brown, stirring after 2 minutes, then stirring every 30 seconds. Allow 2 to 3 minutes for ½ cup almonds or pecans, 2 to 3 minutes for 1 cup almonds, 3 to 4 minutes for 1 cup pecans, 3 to 4 minutes for ½ cup raw peanuts or walnuts, and 3½ to 5 minutes for 1 cup raw peanuts or walnuts. Allow to cool on paper towels. Nuts will continue to toast as they stand.

chocolate-peppermint sandwich cookies

total prep: 15 minutes

Here's a three-step, three-ingredient recipe that couldn't be easier. Try another flavored frosting, such as chocolate, and add crushed cherry-flavored hard candies. Or, experiment with your own favorite flavors.

½ **cup of canned vanilla or reduced-calorie vanilla frosting**

3 **tablespoons finely crushed striped round peppermint candies**

44 **chocolate wafers**

1. In a small mixing bowl stir together the frosting and crushed peppermint candies.

2. Spread 1 level teaspoon frosting mixture on flat side of 22 chocolate wafers.

3. Top with the remaining chocolate wafers, flat side toward frosting mixture. Makes 22 cookies.

Nutrition Facts per cookie: 84 calories, 3 g total fat (1 g saturated fat), 0 mg cholesterol, 76 mg sodium, 14 g carbohydrate, 0 g fiber, 1 g protein.

peanut butter-oatmeal cookies

total prep: 15 minutes

When you need a quick hit for a bake sale or potluck picnic, these gooey, chewy marshmallow drop cookies fill the bill.

1½ cups tiny marshmallows
½ cup peanut butter
¼ cup butter

1½ cups quick-cooking rolled oats
½ cup coconut

1. In a medium saucepan combine marshmallows, peanut butter, and butter. Heat and stir over medium heat until marshmallows melt.

2. Remove from heat and stir in oats and coconut.

3. Quickly drop by rounded teaspoons onto waxed paper. Cool. Cover and store in the refrigerator. Makes about 30 cookies.

Nutrition Facts per cookie: 65 calories, 4 g total fat
(2 g saturated fat), 4 mg cholesterol, 37 mg sodium,
6 g carbohydrate, 1 g fiber, 2 g protein.

child's play

Making cookies is a great way to introduce children to the joys of cooking. Try these tips to make cooking in the kitchen a pleasant experience:

• Let children choose their jobs and how much they want to help.
• Clear a large area in which to work. A small confined area may cause unnecessary accidents to happen.
• Choose simple jobs for smaller children. For example, placing candies onto cookies after baking or decorating baked cookies is an easy job for first-time helpers.
• Allow your children to be artistic. This is supposed to be fun; let your helpers be creative.

chocolate-oatmeal cookies

total prep: 25 minutes   **standing time:** 15 minutes

These rich chocolate cookies get a nutty flavor from the chocolate hazelnut spread. You'll find it next to the peanut butter at the store. If you prefer the flavor of peanut butter and chocolate, use peanut butter instead.

2 cups sugar
¼ cup unsweetened cocoa powder
½ cup milk
½ cup butter

1 tablespoon light corn syrup
¼ cup chocolate hazelnut spread or
    peanut butter
2 cups quick-cooking rolled oats

1. In a heavy saucepan stir together the sugar and cocoa powder; stir in the milk. Add the butter and corn syrup. Bring mixture to boiling, stirring occasionally. Boil mixture, uncovered, for 3 minutes.

2. Stir in the chocolate hazelnut spread or peanut butter until smooth. Stir in the rolled oats until combined.

3. Return the mixture to boiling. Remove saucepan from heat. Using a wooden spoon, beat the mixture until slightly thickened. Let stand 15 to 20 minutes or until the mixture mounds.

4. Drop mixture from a teaspoon onto waxed paper. Cool. Makes about 36 cookies.

Nutrition Facts per cookie: 97 calories, 3 g total fat (2 g saturated fat), / mg cholesterol, 30 mg sodium, 16 g carbohydrate, 0 g fiber, 1 g protein.

so-easy slice

chocolate ribbon cookies

prep: 30 minutes   **bake:** 10 minutes   **oven:** 375°

These striped cookies go as well with a glass of milk as they do with a demitasse of espresso.

½ cup butter	1 teaspoon vanilla
½ cup shortening	3 cups all-purpose flour
1 cup sugar	⅓ cup semisweet chocolate pieces, melted and cooled
½ teaspoon baking soda	
⅛ teaspoon salt	½ cup finely chopped nuts
1 egg	½ cup miniature semisweet chocolate pieces
2 tablespoons milk	¼ teaspoon rum flavoring

1. In a mixing bowl beat butter and shortening with an electric mixer on medium to high speed for 30 seconds. Add sugar, baking soda, and salt; beat until combined. Beat in the egg, milk, and vanilla. Beat in as much of the flour as you can with the mixer. Stir in remaining flour.

2. Divide dough in half. Knead the melted chocolate and nuts into half of the dough. Knead the miniature chocolate pieces and rum flavoring into the other half of dough. Divide each portion of dough in half.

3. To shape dough, line the bottom and sides of a 9x5x3 inch loaf pan with waxed paper or clear plastic wrap. Press half the chocolate dough evenly in pan. Top with half the vanilla dough, then the remaining chocolate dough, then the remaining vanilla dough, pressing each layer firmly and evenly over the last layer (see photos, *opposite page*).

4. Invert pan to remove dough. Peel off waxed paper or plastic wrap. Cut dough crosswise into thirds (see photos, *opposite page*). Slice each third crosswise into ¼-inch-thick slices. Place cookies 2 inches apart on an ungreased cookie sheet.

5. Bake cookies in a 375° oven about 10 minutes or until edges are firm and bottoms are lightly browned. Transfer the cookies to a wire rack; cool. Makes about 54 cookies.

Nutrition Facts per cookie: 100 calories, 6 g total fat (2 g saturated fat), 7 mg cholesterol, 31 mg sodium, 10 g carbohydrate, 1 g fiber, 1 g protein.

& bake

No matter how you cut 'em, slice and bake cookies are great because you can keep them in the freezer and pull them out for a last-minute cookie craving.

spiral cookies

prep: 40 minutes   **chill:** 2 hours   **bake:** 8 minutes   **oven:** 375°

Make a batch of dough for these whimsical pink-and-white spirals and chill it overnight. When company comes, just slice and bake them while you're making tea. You'll have pretty cookies to serve warm from the oven.

1 cup butter	1 egg
1½ cups sugar	1 teaspoon vanilla
1½ teaspoons baking powder	½ teaspoon peppermint extract (optional)
½ teaspoon salt	2½ cups all-purpose flour
	Red paste food coloring

1. In a large mixing bowl beat butter with an electric mixer on medium to high speed 30 seconds. Add the sugar, baking powder, and salt. Beat until combined. Beat in the egg, vanilla, and, if desired peppermint extract. Beat in as much of the flour as you can with the mixer. Stir in remaining flour.

2. Divide dough in half. Tint one portion of the dough with paste food coloring. Knead coloring into dough until well mixed. If necessary, wrap dough in waxed paper or clear plastic wrap and chill in the refrigerator for 1 hour or until easy to handle.

3. On a lightly floured surface, roll each color of dough into a 12x8-inch rectangle (¼- to ⅛-inch thick). Using a large spatula and your hands, place one rectangle on top of the other (see photos, *opposite page*). Press down gently with your hands to seal. Tightly roll up, jelly-roll style, starting from one of the long sides (see photos, *below*). Wrap in waxed paper or clear plastic wrap. Chill in the refrigerator 2 to 4 hours or until firm.

4. Using a sharp knife, cut log into ¼-inch-thick slices. Place slices about 1 inch apart on an ungreased cookie sheet. Bake cookies in a 375° oven for 8 to 10 minutes or until edges are firm and lightly browned. Cool on cookie sheet for 1 minute. Transfer cookies to a wire rack; cool. Makes about 48 cookies.

Nutrition Facts per cookie: 81 calories, 4 g total fat (2 g saturated fat), 15 mg cholesterol, 63 mg sodium, 11 g carbohydrate, 0 g fiber, 1 g protein.

brown sugar-brickle rounds

prep: 30 minutes **chill:** 4 hours **bake:** 10 minutes **oven:** 350°

Brown sugar makes these cookies soft and moist. The almond brickle pieces add a contrasting crunch.

½ cup butter
½ cup shortening
1 cup packed brown sugar
½ teaspoon baking powder
½ teaspoon baking soda
¼ teaspoon salt

1 egg
2 tablespoons milk
½ teaspoon almond extract
3 cups all-purpose flour
1 7½-ounce package (1⅓ cups) almond
   brickle pieces

1. In a large mixing bowl beat butter and shortening with an electric mixer on medium to high speed for 30 seconds. Add the brown sugar, baking powder, baking soda, and salt. Beat until combined, scraping sides of bowl occasionally. Beat in egg, milk, and almond extract until combined. Beat in as much of the flour as you can with the mixer. Stir in almond brickle pieces and remaining flour.

2. Shape dough into two 10-inch-long rolls. Wrap in plastic wrap or waxed paper; chill in refrigerator at least 4 hours or up to 24 hours or until firm enough to slice.

3. Cut rolls into ½-inch-thick slices. Place 2 inches apart on an ungreased cookie sheet. Bake cookies in a 350° oven for 10 to 11 minutes or until edges are firm. Transfer cookies to a wire rack; cool. Makes about 36 cookies.

Nutrition Facts per cookie: 135 calories, 8 g total fat (2 g saturated fat), 15 mg cholesterol, 100 mg sodium, 16 g carbohydrate, 0 g fiber, 1 g protein.

great sliced cookies

To ensure success when making sliced cookies, follow these simple tips:

• Finely chop any nuts or fruit that you add to the dough so it will slice easily.
• Cut the chilled dough with a thin, sharp knife, wiping the knife occasionally with a clean paper towel.
• Occasionally turn the roll of dough while you slice it to get nice round slices. This prevents flattening on one side of the roll.
• Bake sliced cookies until the edges are firm and the bottoms are just lightly browned.

chocolate-coconut spirals

prep: 40 minutes   **chill:** 4 hours   **bake:** 8 minutes   **oven:** 375°

To the cookie that has everything—chocolate, nuts, and cream cheese—we've added coconut, too. Sometimes, nothing impresses like excess.

1 3-ounce package cream cheese, softened	1 cup sugar
⅓ cup sugar	½ teaspoon baking soda
1 teaspoon vanilla	1 egg
1 cup shredded coconut	1 tablespoon milk
½ cup finely chopped nuts	¼ cup unsweetened cocoa powder
⅓ cup butter	1½ cups all-purpose flour

1. For filling, in a small mixing bowl beat cream cheese, the ⅓ cup sugar, and the vanilla with an electric mixer on medium to high speed until smooth. Stir in coconut and nuts; set aside.

2. In a large mixing bowl beat butter on medium to high speed for 30 seconds. Add the 1 cup sugar and the baking soda. Beat until combined, scraping sides of bowl occasionally. Beat in egg and milk. Beat in cocoa powder and as much of the flour as you can with the mixer. Stir in remaining flour.

3. Roll half of the dough between 2 sheets of waxed paper into a 10x8-inch rectangle. Remove top sheet of waxed paper. Spread half of the filling over the dough. Roll up, jelly-roll style, starting from one of the long sides. Moisten the edges with water; pinch to seal. Wrap dough in waxed paper. Repeat with the remaining dough and filling. Chill in the refrigerator for at least 4 hours or up to 24 hours.

4. Grease a cookie sheet. Cut dough into ¼-inch-thick slices. Place the slices 1 inch apart on prepared cookie sheet. Bake cookies in a 375° oven for 8 minutes or until edges are firm. Transfer the cookies to a wire rack; cool. Makes 72 cookies.

Nutrition Facts per cookie: 47 calories, 2 g total fat
(1 g saturated fat), 7 mg cholesterol, 22 mg sodium,
6 g carbohydrate, 0 g fiber, 1 g protein.

apricot spirals

prep: 40 minutes   **chill:** 1 hour   **bake:** 9 minutes   **oven:** 375°

Fresh apricots don't have to be in season to make these cookies. Tart dried apricots make up the spiral filling, giving the cookies a flavorful touch of summer that you can enjoy year-round.

¾ cup butter
1 cup sugar
1 teaspoon baking powder

1 egg
2¼ cups all-purpose flour
1 recipe Apricot Filling

1. In a large mixing bowl beat butter with an electric mixer on medium to high speed for 30 seconds. Add the sugar and baking powder. Beat until combined, scraping sides of bowl occasionally. Beat in egg. Beat in as much of the flour as you can with the mixer. Stir in remaining flour. (Dough will be stiff.)

2. On a lightly floured surface, roll the dough to a 16x12-inch rectangle. Spread Apricot Filling almost to edges. Roll up, jelly-roll style, starting from one of the long sides. Pinch to seal. Cut roll in half crosswise. Wrap in plastic wrap or waxed paper; chill for 1 to 2 hours.

3. Lightly grease a cookie sheet. Remove one roll from the refrigerator. Unwrap and reshape slightly, if necessary. Cut roll into ¼-inch-thick slices. Place slices about 2 inches apart on prepared cookie sheet. Bake in a

375° oven for 9 to 11 minutes or until edges are lightly browned. Transfer cookies to a wire rack; cool. Repeat with remaining dough. Makes about 55 to 60 cookies.

Apricot Filling: In a small saucepan combine ⅔ cup finely snipped dried apricots and ½ cup water. Bring to boiling; reduce heat. Simmer, covered, about 15 minutes or until water is nearly absorbed and the apricots are tender. Do not drain. Mash apricots slightly; stir in ⅓ cup packed brown sugar. Cover and cool.

Nutrition Facts per cookie: 64 calories, 3 g total fat (1 g saturated fat), 7 mg cholesterol, 32 mg sodium, 10 g carbohydrate, 0 g fiber, 1 g protein.

brown sugar-hazelnut cookies

prep: 30 minutes   **chill:** 4 hours   **bake:** 10 minutes   **oven:** 375°

Either light or dark brown sugar works equally well in most recipes. Dark sugar makes a slightly darker cookie that bakes up a bit softer with a stronger hint of molasses flavor.

½ cup shortening
½ cup butter
1¼ cups packed brown sugar
½ teaspoon baking soda
¼ teaspoon salt
1 egg
1 teaspoon vanilla

¾ cup toasted ground hazelnuts or pecans
2½ cups all-purpose flour
⅓ cup toasted finely chopped hazelnuts or
      pecans (optional)
    Milk chocolate, melted (optional)
    Toasted, finely chopped hazelnuts or
      almonds (optional)

1. In a large mixing bowl beat shortening and butter with an electric mixer on medium to high speed for 30 seconds. Add the brown sugar, baking soda, and salt. Beat until combined, scraping sides of bowl occasionally. Beat in the egg and vanilla until combined. Beat in as much of the flour as you can. Stir in the remaining flour and the ¾ cup ground nuts.

2. Divide dough in half. On waxed paper, shape each half of dough into a 10-inch-long roll. Lift and smooth the waxed paper to help shape the roll. If desired, roll one of the logs in the ⅓ cup chopped nuts. Wrap each in waxed paper or plastic wrap. Chill in the refrigerator for at least 4 hours or until firm enough to slice. (Or, wrap dough in foil and freeze for up to 3 months; thaw in the refrigerator before slicing and baking.)

3. Cut rolls into ¼-inch-thick slices. Place slices 1 inch apart on ungreased cookie sheets. Bake in a 375° oven 10 minutes or until edges are firm. Transfer cookies to a wire rack; cool.

4. To decorate with melted chocolate, dip cookies without nuts on the edges in melted chocolate, dipping about half of the cookie. Or, drizzle melted chocolate over cookies (with or without nuts on edges). Sprinkle with some of the finely chopped nuts. Makes 60 cookies.

Nutrition Facts per plain cookie: 74 calories, 4 g total fat (1 g saturated fat), 4 mg cholesterol, 40 mg sodium, 8 g carbohydrate, 0 g fiber, 1 g protein.

butterfly cookies

prep: 40 minutes   **bake:** 6 minutes   **oven:** 375°

Translucent colors of candied fruit adorn the wings of these imaginative cookie gems—pretty enough for any May basket.

¾ cup butter	1 egg
½ cup granulated sugar	½ teaspoon almond extract
¼ cup packed brown sugar	1¾ cups all-purpose flour
¼ teaspoon baking powder	½ cup chopped candied pineapple
⅛ teaspoon baking soda	½ cup chopped candied papaya
⅛ teaspoon salt	¼ cup semisweet chocolate pieces
	¼ teaspoon shortening

1. In a large mixing bowl beat butter with an electric mixer on medium to high speed for 30 seconds. Add granulated sugar, brown sugar, baking powder, baking soda, and salt. Beat until combined. Beat in egg and almond extract. Beat in as much of the flour as you can with the mixer. Stir in candied pineapple, candied papaya, and remaining flour.

2. If dough is too sticky to handle, cover and chill dough in refrigerator for 1 to 2 hours or until easy to handle. Divide dough in half. Shape each half into a 9-inch-long roll. (If desired, wrap rolls in freezer paper. Store dough in the freezer for up to 6 months. For easier slicing, let the rolls of dough thaw in the refrigerator several hours before slicing and baking.)

3. To bake, cut rolls into ¼-inch-thick slices. Cut each slice in half. Place rounded sides of two halves together on an ungreased cookie sheet, forming a butterfly. (See photos, at *right*.)

Bake cookies in a 375° oven about 6 minutes or until the edges just begin to brown. Transfer the cookies to wire racks; cool.

4. In a small saucepan combine chocolate and shortening; heat and stir over low heat until melted. Let cool slightly. Spoon into a small, self-sealing plastic bag; seal bag. Snip a tiny piece off one corner of the bag. Pipe a chocolate body onto each cookie. Makes about 60 cookies.

Nutrition Facts per cookie: 56 calories, 3 g total fat
(1 g saturated fat), 7 mg cholesterol, 32 mg sodium,
7 g carbohydrate, 0 g fiber, 0 g protein.

butterscotch **bites**

prep: 40 minutes   **chill:** 4 hours   **bake:** 8 minutes   **oven:** 350°

If your little tykes love tea parties, they'll love serving these sweet treats to their guests. If you like, freeze the baked cookies to have on hand for an impromptu tea party (see page 5 for freezing directions).

1 cup butter
1 cup packed brown sugar

½ cup butterscotch-flavored pieces, melted and cooled
1 teaspoon vanilla
2½ cups all-purpose flour

1. In a large mixing bowl beat butter with an electric mixer on medium to high speed for 30 seconds. Add the brown sugar, melted butterscotch pieces, and vanilla. Beat until combined. Beat in as much flour as you can with the mixer. Stir in remaining flour. Divide the dough into 4 portions.

2. Shape each portion into a 9-inch-long roll. Wrap the rolls in waxed paper or clear plastic wrap. Chill in refrigerator for at least 4 hours or up to 48 hours.

3. Cut dough into ¼-inch-thick slices. Place slices 1 inch apart on an ungreased cookie sheet. Bake cookies in a 350° oven for 8 to 10 minutes or until edges are set.

4. Cool on cookie sheet for 1 minute. Transfer cookies to a wire rack; cool. Makes about 110 cookies.

Nutrition Facts per cookie: 34 calories, 2 g total fat
(1 g saturated fat), 4 mg cholesterol, 18 mg sodium,
4 g carbohydrate, 0 g fiber, 0 g protein.

molasses slices

prep: 30 minutes   **chill:** 6 hours   **bake:** 8 minutes   **oven:** 375°

Molasses cookies are one of the earliest American originals. Add this recipe to your trove of family favorites.

½ cup shortening
½ cup butter
¾ cup sugar
1½ teaspoons baking soda
½ teaspoon ground cinnamon
¼ teaspoon ground nutmeg

¼ teaspoon ground ginger
¼ teaspoon ground cloves
1 egg
½ cup molasses
2¼ cups all-purpose flour

1. In a large mixing bowl beat shortening and butter with an electric mixer on medium to high speed for 30 seconds. Add the sugar, baking soda, cinnamon, nutmeg, ginger, and cloves. Beat until combined, scraping sides of bowl occasionally. Beat in egg and molasses. Beat in as much of the flour as you can with the mixer. Stir in remaining flour.

2. Cover and chill dough in refrigerator for 2 hours or until easy to handle. Divide dough in half. Shape each half into a 9-inch-long roll. Wrap rolls in plastic wrap or waxed paper. Chill in the refrigerator for at least 4 hours or up to 24 hours.

3. Cut rolls into ¼-inch-thick slices. Place slices about 2 inches apart on an ungreased cookie sheet. Bake cookies in a 375° oven about 8 minutes or until edges are firm. Cool on cookie sheet for 2 minutes. Transfer cookies to a wire rack; cool. Makes about 54 cookies.

Nutrition Facts per cookie: 69 calories, 4 g total fat (2 g saturated fat), 8 mg cholesterol, 54 mg sodium, 8 g carbohydrate, 0 g fiber, 1 g protein.

spice is nice

Throw out your old spices! It's a shame to ruin a great recipe by using spices that have been sitting in your pantry for ages. The flavors in spices come from their volatile oils, which begin to "go off," or deteriorate, as soon as the whole spice is ground. Spices that have lost their punch can give baked goods a bitter or medicinal taste. Follow these tips for using spices:

• Keep all spices well-sealed in an airtight container.
• Store spices in a cool, dry place.
• Buy spices in small amounts and throw out any spices older than 6 months.
• Grind whole spices just before you need them to ensure the freshest flavor.

brownie nut slices

prep: 30 minutes   **chill:** 5 hours   **bake:** 10 minutes   **oven:** 375°

All the flavor of an old-fashioned fudge brownie is baked into these cookies. Keep the dough in the freezer for those chocolate cookie urges. Just remember to thaw the dough in the refrigerator several hours for easier slicing.

1 cup butter	4 ounces semisweet chocolate, melted and cooled
1½ cups sugar	1 teaspoon vanilla
1 teaspoon baking powder	2½ cups all-purpose flour
¼ teaspoon baking soda	Milk
⅛ teaspoon salt	¾ cup finely chopped walnuts
1 egg	

1. In a large mixing bowl beat butter with an electric mixer on medium to high speed for 30 seconds. Add sugar, baking powder, baking soda, and salt. Beat until combined. Beat in egg, chocolate, and vanilla. Beat in as much of the flour as you can with the mixer. Stir in remaining flour.

2. If dough is too sticky to handle, cover and chill dough for 1 to 2 hours until easy to handle. Divide dough into 3 equal portions. Shape each portion into an 8½-inch-long roll. Brush rolls with milk; roll in walnuts. Wrap in waxed paper or plastic wrap. Chill in the refrigerator for at least 4 hours or up to 48 hours.

3. To bake, cut the rolls into ⅜-inch-thick slices. Place 1 inch apart on an ungreased cookie sheet. Bake in a 375° oven about 10 minutes or until edges are set. Cool on cookie sheet for 1 minute. Transfer cookies to wire racks; cool. Makes 60 cookies.

Nutrition Facts per cookie: 86 calories, 5 g total fat (1 g saturated fat), 8 mg cholesterol, 45 mg sodium, 10 g carbohydrate, 0 g fiber, 1 g protein.

margarine in cookies

If you choose to make cookies with margarine rather than butter, the firmness of the cookie dough may vary depending on the type of margarine. Be sure to choose a stick product that's labeled "margarine" not "spread." It should contain at least 60 percent vegetable oil. A 100 percent corn-oil margarine will produce a soft dough (see tip box, Best Bet: Butter, page 92). So, you would need to adjust the recipe chilling instructions. You can quick-freeze cookies made with margarine for about one-third of the refrigerator chilling time. (Do not quick-freeze dough made with butter; it will become too firm to work with.) For shaped or sliced cookies, chill the dough in the freezer instead of the refrigerator; for cutout cookies, refrigerate the dough at least 5 hours.

praline rounds

prep: 45 minutes   **chill:** 4 hours   **bake:** 8 minutes   **oven:** 375°

This pecan praline cookie defines Southern hospitality in every delicious bite. The brown sugar frosting is the key to the cookies' taste resemblance to the classic Southern candies.

½ cup butter
½ cup shortening
1 cup packed brown sugar
½ teaspoon baking powder
¼ teaspoon baking soda
¼ teaspoon salt

1 egg
2 tablespoons milk
1 teaspoon vanilla
3 cups all-purpose flour
1 cup finely chopped pecans
1 recipe Brown Sugar Frosting

1. In a large bowl beat butter and shortening with an electric mixer on medium to high speed for 30 seconds. Add brown sugar, baking powder, baking soda, and salt. Beat until combined. Beat in egg, milk, and vanilla. Beat in as much of the flour as you can with the mixer. Stir in ½ cup of the pecans and the remaining flour. Divide dough in half. Shape each half into a 10-inch long roll. Wrap in waxed paper or plastic wrap. Chill in the refrigerator for at least 4 hours or up to 48 hours.

2. Cut the dough into ¼-inch-thick slices. Place about 2 inches apart on an ungreased cookie sheet. Bake cookies in a 375° oven for 8 to 10 minutes or until edges are firm.

3. Transfer to a wire rack; cool. Drizzle with warm Brown Sugar Frosting. Sprinkle with remaining pecans. Makes about 72 cookies.

Brown Sugar Frosting: In a small saucepan combine 1 cup packed brown sugar, ¼ cup butter, and ¼ cup half-and-half or light cream. Heat and stir over medium heat until mixture comes to a full boil. Boil 1 minute, stirring constantly. Remove from heat. Add 1⅓ cups sifted powdered sugar. Beat with a wire whisk or fork until smooth. (Frosting will thicken as it cools. If necessary, add a few drops of water to make of drizzling consistency.)

Nutrition Facts per cookie: 90 calories, 5 g total fat
(1 g saturated fat), 6 mg cholesterol, 36 mg sodium,
12 g carbohydrate, 0 g fiber, 1 g protein.

holiday

marbled holiday cutouts

prep: 1 hour   **chill:** 2 hours   **bake:** 7 minutes   **oven:** 375°

Simply marble-ous! These cardamom-laced cutouts are a colorful addition to any cookie platter.

½ cup butter
1 cup sugar
1 teaspoon baking powder
1 teaspoon finely shredded orange peel
¼ teaspoon baking soda
¼ teaspoon ground cardamom or
    ground nutmeg

⅛ teaspoon salt
1 egg
½ cup dairy sour cream
1 teaspoon vanilla
2½ cups all-purpose flour
    Assorted paste or liquid food coloring
    Confectionary pearl sugar or colored sugar (optional)

1. In a large mixing bowl beat butter with an electric mixer on medium to high speed for 30 seconds. Add sugar, baking powder, orange peel, baking soda, cardamom or nutmeg, and salt. Beat until combined. Beat in egg, sour cream, and vanilla. Beat in as much of the flour as you can with the mixer. Stir in remaining flour.

2. Divide dough in half. Wrap half of the dough in waxed paper or plastic wrap and refrigerate. Divide the remaining dough into 4 portions. Place each portion in a bowl. Add food coloring to each portion as desired, stirring until dough is evenly colored. Wrap each portion of dough in waxed paper or plastic wrap. Chill dough at least 2 hours or up to 24 hours.

3. On a lightly floured surface, form a mound by dropping small amounts of each of the doughs close together in a random pattern (use half of the plain dough and half of each of the colored doughs). Shape the mound into a ball (see photos, *opposite page*). Cover and refrigerate; repeat with remaining doughs. On a lightly floured surface, roll 1 ball of dough to ⅛ to ¼ inch thickness. Using 2- to 3-inch cookie cutters, cut dough into desired shapes. Place cutouts 1 inch apart on an ungreased cookie sheet. If desired, sprinkle with pearl or colored sugars. (Reroll scraps of dough only once. Overworking dough blurs the colors.) Repeat with the other ball of dough.

4. Bake cookies in a 375° oven for 7 to 8 minutes or until edges are firm and bottoms are very lightly browned. Transfer cookies to a wire rack; cool. Makes about 54 cookies.

Nutrition Facts per cookie: 55 calories, 2 g total fat (1 g saturated fat), 9 mg cholesterol, 37 mg sodium, 8 g carbohydrate, 0 g fiber, 1 g protein.

treasures

Long-time favorite recipes make a showing during holiday celebrations—and cookies top that list of must-haves. Here you'll find a trove of some of the best cookies for any holiday.

christmas ribbons

prep: 30 minutes **bake:** 6 minutes **oven:** 375°

Bedeck your Christmas party with these crisp cookie ribbons of pink and green. You also can use raffia or ribbon to carefully tie several in a bundle and display them upright in a decorative canister.

1½ cups butter
1 cup sugar
1 teaspoon baking powder
1 egg

2 teaspoons vanilla
½ teaspoon lemon or orange extract
3½ cups all-purpose flour
    Red and green food coloring

1. In a large mixing bowl beat butter with an electric mixer on medium to high speed for 30 seconds. Add sugar and baking powder. Beat until combined. Beat in egg, vanilla, and lemon or orange extract. Beat in as much of the flour as you can with the mixer. Stir in remaining flour.

2. Divide dough into 3 portions. Using a few drops of red food coloring, tint one portion of dough pink. Using a few drops of green food coloring, tint a second portion of dough light green. Leave the third portion plain. Do not chill dough.

3. Pack dough into a cookie press, placing pink dough on one side, green on the other, and plain in the center. Using the ribbon plate, force dough through press onto ungreased cookie sheets. Cut into 2- to 3-inch lengths.

4. Bake cookies in a 375° oven for 6 to 8 minutes or until edges of cookies are firm but not brown. Transfer cookies to a wire rack; cool. Makes about 60 cookies.

Nutrition Facts per cookie: 81 calories, 5 g total fat (1 g saturated fat), 10 mg cholesterol, 49 mg sodium, 9 g carbohydrate, 0 g fiber, 1 g protein.

cookie storage

To preserve the just-baked freshness of cookies, choose tightly covered containers or plastic bags. Either choice will prevent humidity from softening crisp cookies and air from drying out soft cookies. Be sure to store crisp and soft cookies separately. Most cookies can be stored successfully for up to three days at room temperature.

To freeze cookies, place unfrosted cookies in freezer bags or airtight freezer containers for up to 8 months. Before serving, thaw cookies at room temperature for 15 minutes. Frost, if desired.

shortbread sticks

prep: 25 minutes   **bake:** 20 minutes   **oven:** 325°

These festive shortbread cookies sparkle with colorful candied fruits and peels. One end of each cookie is dipped into either white chocolate or semisweet chocolate, whichever you prefer.

1¼ cups all-purpose flour
 3 tablespoons brown sugar
 ½ cup butter
 ¼ cup finely chopped mixed candied fruits and peels
      or candied red and/or green cherries

 ½ teaspoon vanilla
 3 ounces white chocolate baking squares
      or semisweet chocolate
 2 teaspoons shortening
 ¼ cup finely chopped pecans, walnuts, or
      mixed nuts

1. In a medium mixing bowl combine the flour and brown sugar. Using a pastry blender, cut in butter until the mixture resembles fine crumbs and starts to cling. Stir in the candied fruits. Sprinkle with the vanilla. Form the mixture into a ball and knead until smooth.

2. On a lightly floured surface, roll the dough to an 8x6-inch rectangle. Using a knife, cut dough in half lengthwise. Cut into 1-inch-wide strips. Place strips 1 inch apart on an ungreased baking sheet.

3. Bake in a 325° oven for 20 to 25 minutes or until bottoms just start to brown. Transfer the cookies to a wire rack; cool.

4. In a heavy, small saucepan combine the white chocolate baking squares or semisweet chocolate and shortening; heat and stir over low heat until melted. Dip one end of each cooled cookie into melted chocolate. Place on wire rack. Before chocolate sets, sprinkle chocolate-coated end with nuts. Let cookies stand until chocolate is set. Makes 16 cookies.

Nutrition Facts per cookie: 146 calories, 9 g total fat (5 g saturated fat), 17 mg cholesterol, 64 mg sodium, 14 g carbohydrate, 0 g fiber, 2 g protein.

sour cream snowflakes

prep: 30 minutes   **chill:** 1 hour   **bake:** 7 minutes   **oven:** 375°

Sour cream makes these raspberry-topped snowflakes extra tender. Use several of your favorite jam flavors for a variety of cookies from just one recipe.

½ cup butter
⅓ cup shortening
1 cup granulated sugar
¾ teaspoon baking powder
¼ teaspoon baking soda
⅓ cup dairy sour cream

1 egg
1 teaspoon vanilla
2½ cups all-purpose flour
⅓ cup raspberry jam
    Sifted powdered sugar

1. In a large mixing bowl beat butter and shortening with an electric mixer on medium to high speed for 30 seconds. Add granulated sugar, baking powder, and baking soda. Beat until combined. Beat in the sour cream, egg, and vanilla. Beat in as much of the flour as you can with the mixer. Stir in remaining flour. Divide dough in half. Cover and chill dough in refrigerator for 1 to 2 hours or until easy to handle.

2. On a lightly floured surface, roll half of the dough to ⅛-inch thickness. Using a 2½-inch star-shaped cookie cutter, cut into stars. Cut a small star shape from the center of half of the stars. Place cookies on ungreased cookie sheet.

3. Bake cookies in a 375° oven for 7 to 8 minutes or until edges are firm and bottoms are very lightly browned. Transfer cookies to a wire rack; cool.

4. Spread the center of half of the cookies with jam, using about ¼ teaspoon of jam on each. Place a second cookie on top, offsetting the points of the top and bottom cookies. Sprinkle cookies with powdered sugar. Makes 48 cookies.

Nutrition Facts per cookie: 79 calories, 4 g total fat (2 g saturated fat), 10 mg cholesterol, 34 mg sodium, 10 g carbohydrate, 0 g fiber, 1 g protein.

chocolate mint creams

prep: 30 minutes   **chill:** 1 hour   **bake:** 10 minutes   **oven:** 350°

Convenient and easy, melted mint kisses are the icing on the cookie for this indulgent recipe.

1¼ cups all-purpose flour
½ teaspoon baking soda
1 6-ounce package (1 cup) semisweet
     chocolate pieces

⅔ cup packed brown sugar
6 tablespoons butter
1 tablespoon water
1 egg
8 to 12 ounces pastel cream mint kisses

1. In a small bowl stir together flour and baking soda; set aside. In a medium saucepan combine chocolate pieces, brown sugar, butter, and water. Heat and stir over low heat until chocolate is melted. Pour into a large mixing bowl; let stand for 10 to 15 minutes or until cool.

2. Beat egg into chocolate mixture. Stir in flour mixture until well mixed (dough will be soft). Cover and chill in the refrigerator for 1 to 2 hours or until easy to handle.

3. Shape dough into 1-inch balls. Place 2 inches apart on an ungreased cookie sheet. Bake cookies in a 350° oven for 8 minutes.

4. Remove cookies from oven and immediately top each cookie with a mint. Return to the oven and bake about 2 minutes more or until bottoms are lightly browned. Swirl melted mints with a knife to frost cookies. Transfer cookies to a wire rack; cool until mints are firm. Makes about 48 cookies.

Nutrition Facts per cookie: 69 calories, 3 g total fat
(1 g saturated fat), 6 mg cholesterol, 29 mg sodium,
9 g carbohydrate, 1 g fiber, 1 g protein.

best bet: butter

All of the recipes in this cookbook call for butter rather than margarine. In cookies, butter gives a wonderful flavor but also ensures good results. Many margarines found at the supermarket today contain more water than oil, which will give you undesirable baking results. If you choose to use margarine instead of butter, be sure to use only a stick margarine that contains at least 60 to 80 percent vegetable oil (oil content is listed on the package). Stick margarines will also produce a soft dough, so you may need to chill the dough longer than directed in the recipes. Soft, spreadable margarines have a high water content and can cause the cookie dough—and your cookies—to be wet and tough but will dry out faster. Diet, whipped, liquid, and soft spreads or margarines are for table use—not baking.

sandies

prep: 30 minutes   **bake:** 20 minutes   **oven:** 325°

These buttery cookies been a favorite of the Better Homes and Gardens® test kitchen for years. Shape the cookies into crescents or just into balls. The powdered sugar coating makes them melt in your mouth.

1 cup butter
⅓ cup granulated sugar
1 tablespoon water
1 teaspoon vanilla

2¼ cups all-purpose flour
1 cup chopped pecans
1 cup sifted powdered sugar or
    granulated sugar

1. In a mixing bowl beat butter with an electric mixer on medium to high speed for 30 seconds. Add the granulated sugar, water, and vanilla. Beat until combined. Beat in as much of the flour as you can with a mixer. Stir in remaining flour and the pecans.

2. Shape dough into 1-inch balls or 2x½-inch crescents. Place on an ungreased cookie sheet. Bake cookies in a 325° oven about 20 minutes or until bottoms are lightly browned. Transfer cookies to a wire rack; cool.

3. Place cooled cookies in a bag containing the powdered sugar. Gently shake to coat. Makes about 36 cookies.

Nutrition Facts per cookie: 111 calories, 7 g total fat
(2 g saturated fat), 7 mg cholesterol, 47 mg sodium,
11 g carbohydrate, 0 g fiber, 1 g protein.

peppermint eggnog wreaths

prep: 30 minutes   **chill:** 30 minutes   **bake:** 8 minutes   **oven:** 375°

Two great holiday tastes—peppermint and eggnog—intertwine to make holiday wreaths. Use green food coloring to make wreaths with other color combinations.

¾ **cup butter**
¾ **cup sugar**
¼ **teaspoon baking powder**
¼ **teaspoon salt**
1 **egg**
⅓ **cup dairy eggnog**

1 **teaspoon vanilla**
2½ **cups all-purpose flour**
¼ **teaspoon peppermint extract**
¼ **teaspoon red paste food coloring**
¼ **teaspoon green paste food coloring**
  Purchased vanilla frosting (optional)

1. In a large mixing bowl beat the butter with an electric mixer on medium to high speed for 30 seconds. Add the sugar, baking powder, and salt. Beat until combined. Beat in the egg, eggnog, and vanilla. Beat in as much of the flour as you can with the mixer. Stir in remaining flour.

2. Place half of the dough in a small bowl. Stir in the peppermint extract and red food coloring. Stir the green food coloring into the remaining plain dough. Cover and chill both portions of dough in the refrigerator for 30 minutes or until easy to handle.

3. On a lightly floured surface, shape each dough portion into a 12-inch-long log. Cut each log into twenty-four ½-inch-thick pieces. Roll each piece into a 6-inch-long rope (see photos, *opposite page*). (If dough is too soft and difficult to work with, cover and chill the ropes for 10 to 15 minutes.)

4. Place a red and a green rope side by side; twist together 5 or 6 times. Shape the twisted rope into a circle, gently pinching together the ends where they meet (see photos, *below*). Place 2 inches apart on an ungreased cookie sheet. Repeat with remaining dough.

5. Bake cookies in a 375° oven for 8 to 10 minutes or until the edges are lightly browned. Cool on cookie sheet for 1 minute. Transfer cookies to a wire rack; cool.

6. Fill a decorating bag fitted with a round tip with purchased frosting. Pipe a ribbon with streamers at the top of each wreath. Let cookies stand until frosting is set. Makes 24 cookies.

Nutrition Facts per cookie: 152 calories, 6 g total fat
(4 g saturated fat), 24 mg cholesterol, 90 mg sodium,
22 g carbohydrate, 0 g fiber, 2 g protein.

frosties

prep: 40 minutes   **bake:** 18 minutes   **oven:** 325°

Frosty the snowman, an ever-popular character at Christmastime, is fun for the kids to make and eat.

1 cup butter	Miniature semisweet chocolate pieces
½ cup sugar	Gumdrops
1 teaspoon vanilla	Rolled fruit leather, cut into 3-inch-long
¼ teaspoon salt	thin strips
2¼ cups all-purpose flour	1 recipe Decorating Icing

1. In a medium mixing bowl beat butter with an electric mixer on medium to high speed for 30 seconds. Add sugar, vanilla, and salt. Beat until combined. Beat in as much of the flour as you can with the mixer. Stir in remaining flour. For each snowman, shape dough into 3 balls: one 1-inch ball, one ¾-inch ball, and one ½-inch ball.

2. Place balls on an ungreased baking sheet in decreasing sizes with edges touching. Press together slightly. For the eyes, insert 2 chocolate pieces in smallest ball. For buttons, place 1 chocolate piece in the middle ball and 2 down the center of largest ball.

3. Bake cookies in a 325° oven for 18 to 20 minutes or until done. Transfer cookies to wire racks; cool.

4. For the hat, flatten a gumdrop to an oval shape (about 1½x1 inches). Roll oval into a cone shape. Pinch the edges. Roll up bottom edge of cone to form hat brim. Attach to head with Decorating Icing. For a scarf, wrap a fruit leather strip around each snowman's neck. Spoon Decorating Icing into a small self-sealing plastic bag; seal bag. Snip a tiny piece off 1 corner of the bag. Pipe brooms and faces on cookies. Makes 24 cookies.

Decorating Icing: Stir together 1 cup sifted powdered sugar and 1 tablespoon milk. Stir in enough additional milk to make frosting of piping consistency. Tint with paste food coloring.

Nutrition Facts per cookie: 162 calories, 9 g total fat (2 g saturated fat), 10 mg cholesterol, 80 mg sodium, 19 g carbohydrate, 1 g fiber, 1 g protein.

nutcracker cookies

prep: 40 minutes **chill:** 2 hours **bake:** 5 minutes **oven:** 375°

Use cookie cutters in the shape of dancers, toy soldiers, dolls, and all the things that remind you of Tchaikovsky's famous ballet. Serve these whole wheat and honey cookies with hot spiced rum or apple cider after enjoying the ballet.

1½ cups all-purpose flour
 1 cup whole wheat flour
 ½ cup butter
 ½ cup packed brown sugar
 ½ teaspoon baking soda

 ½ teaspoon ground cardamom or 1 teaspoon
      ground cinnamon
 1 egg
 ⅓ cup honey
 1 teaspoon vanilla
 1 recipe Meringue Powder Glaze

1. In a medium mixing bowl stir together the all-purpose flour and whole wheat flour; set aside.

2. In a large mixing bowl beat butter with an electric mixer on medium to high speed for 30 seconds. Add the brown sugar, baking soda, and cardamom or cinnamon. Beat until fluffy. Beat in the egg, honey, and vanilla. Beat in as much of the flour mixture as you can with a mixer. Stir in the remaining flour mixture. Divide dough in half. Cover and chill dough in the refrigerator for 2 hours or until dough is easy to handle.

3. On a lightly floured surface, roll dough out to ⅛- to ¼-inch thickness. Cut with assorted cutters. Place on an ungreased cookie sheet about 2 inches apart.

4. Bake cookies in a 375° oven for 5 to 6 minutes or until edges are lightly browned. Transfer immediately to a wire rack; cool. Decorate with Meringue Powder Glaze. Makes about 72 cookies.

Meringue Powder Glaze: In a medium mixing bowl stir together ¼ cup warm water and 2 tablespoons meringue powder. Stir in 2 cups sifted powdered sugar. Gradually stir in about 1½ cups additional sifted powdered sugar to make a smooth glaze that is easy to spread. (The glaze should be fairly thin with a flowing consistency.)

Nutrition Facts per cookie: 55 calories, 1 g total fat (1 g saturated fat), 3 mg cholesterol, 25 mg sodium, 10 g carbohydrate, 0 g fiber, 1 g protein.

swirled mint cookies

prep: 40 minutes   **chill:** 1½ hours   **bake:** 8 minutes   **oven:** 375°

Dress up this model holiday cookie even more by dipping the pressing glass into colored sugar crystals instead of granulated sugar.

1 cup butter	½ teaspoon peppermint extract
1 cup sugar	2 cups all-purpose flour
½ teaspoon baking powder	10 drops red food coloring
1 egg	10 drops green food coloring
1 teaspoon vanilla	Sugar

1. In a large mixing bowl beat butter with an electric mixer on medium to high speed for 30 seconds. Add the 1 cup sugar and the baking powder. Beat until fluffy. Beat in egg, vanilla, and peppermint. Beat in as much of the flour as you can with the mixer. Stir in remaining flour.

2. Divide dough into 3 equal portions. Stir red food coloring into 1 portion, stir green food coloring into a second portion, and leave third portion plain. Cover each portion with foil or plastic wrap and chill in the refrigerator about 1 hour or until easy to handle.

3. Divide each color of dough into 4 equal portions. On a lightly floured surface, roll each portion into a ½-inch-diameter rope. Place a red, a green, and a plain rope side by side. Twist together. Repeat with remaining ropes

(see photos, *opposite page*). Chill twisted ropes for 30 minutes. Cut ropes into ½-inch-thick slices for larger cookies or ¼-inch-thick slices for smaller ones. Carefully roll into balls, blending colors as little as possible. Place balls about 2 inches apart on ungreased cookie sheets. Using a glass dipped in sugar, flatten each ball to ¼-inch thickness (see photos, *below*).

4. Bake cookies in a 375° oven until edges are set (allow 8 to 10 minutes for larger cookies or 6 to 8 minutes for smaller ones). Transfer cookies to wire racks; cool. Makes about 72 large cookies or 144 small cookies.

Nutrition Facts per large cookie: 46 calories, 3 g total fat (2 g saturated fat), 10 mg cholesterol, 29 mg sodium, 5 g carbohydrate, 0 g fiber, 0 g protein.

cocoa-caramel thumbprints

prep: 45 minutes **bake:** 10 minutes **oven:** 375°

The creamy caramel center adds an extra touch of home-for-the-holidays comfort to these soft, festive cookies.

½ cup butter
½ cup shortening
¾ cup sugar
½ teaspoon baking powder
1 egg yolk
1 teaspoon almond extract or vanilla
½ cup unsweetened cocoa powder

1¾ cups all-purpose flour
1 slightly beaten egg white
1½ cups finely chopped almonds or walnuts
20 chocolate or vanilla caramels, unwrapped
(about 7 ounces)
3 tablespoons half-and-half or light cream

1. Grease a cookie sheet; set aside. In a large mixing bowl beat butter and shortening with an electric mixer on medium to high speed for 30 seconds. Add the sugar and baking powder. Beat until combined, scraping sides of bowl occasionally. Beat in the egg yolk and almond extract or vanilla. Beat in the cocoa powder and as much of the flour as you can with the mixer. Stir in remaining flour. If dough is too sticky to handle, cover and chill dough about 1 hour or until easy to handle.

2. Shape dough into 1-inch balls. Roll balls in egg white; roll balls in almonds or walnuts to coat. Place the balls 1 inch apart on the prepared cookie sheet. Press your thumb into the center of each ball. Bake in a 375° oven for 10 to 12 minutes or until edges are firm.

3. Meanwhile, in a small saucepan combine the caramels and half-and-half or light cream. Cook and stir over medium-low heat just until caramels are melted. Remove saucepan from heat.

4. Transfer cookies to a wire rack. Spoon about ½ teaspoon warm caramel mixture into center of each cookie; cool. Makes about 54 cookies.

Nutrition Facts per cookie: 98 calories, 6 g total fat (2 g saturated fat), 9 mg cholesterol, 32 mg sodium, 10 g carbohydrate, 1 g fiber, 2 g protein.

cookie sheet sense

When baking cookies, choose your cookie sheet wisely.

- Light-colored, dull-finished, heavy-gauge cookie sheets are best. Old cookie sheets with darkened surfaces can overbrown the bottoms of cookies. Shiny sheets are best for cookies that should not brown too much on the bottoms, such as shortbreads.
- Insulated cookie sheets are fine for making pale cookies with soft centers. Problems may occur in cookies high in butter, shaped cookies, and some drop cookies because the butter may start to melt, leaking out before the dough sets. If the dough spreads before it sets, the cookies may have thin edges.
- Nonstick cookie sheets are fine to use if you want to skip the greasing step. However, the dough may not spread as much, resulting in a thicker cookie with smooth bottoms.

white chocolate snowcap cookies

prep: 45 minutes   **bake:** 8 minutes/15 minutes   **oven:** 350°/300°

At holiday time or any time, these hidden-treasure treats are surefire crowd-pleasers. What's the treasure? A kiss of chocolate hidden under a crisp cap of meringue.

⅓ cup butter
⅓ cup sugar
1 egg yolk
1 ounce white chocolate baking square,
    melted and cooled
½ teaspoon vanilla

1 cup all-purpose flour
26 to 30 milk chocolate kisses with
    almonds, unwrapped
2 egg whites
½ teaspoon vanilla
¼ teaspoon cream of tartar
3 tablespoons sugar

1. Grease cookie sheet; set aside. In a medium mixing bowl beat butter with an electric mixer on medium to high speed for 30 seconds. Add the ⅓ cup sugar and beat until combined. Beat in the egg yolk, white baking square, and ½ teaspoon vanilla. Beat in as much of the flour as you can with the mixer. Stir in remaining flour.

2. Shape dough into 1 inch balls. Place balls 2 inches apart on prepared cookie sheet. Press to 1½-inch diameter using the bottom of a floured small glass.

3. Bake cookies in a 350° oven about 8 minutes or until edges are set. Cool on cookie sheet for 1 minute. Place 1 chocolate kiss in center of each cookie. Cool cookies on cookie sheet until candy is firm.* Reduce oven temperature to 300°.

4. For the meringue, in a medium mixing bowl beat the egg whites, ½ teaspoon vanilla, and the cream of tartar with an electric mixer on medium speed about 1 minute or until soft peaks form (tips curl). Gradually add the 3 tablespoons sugar, 1 tablespoon at a time, beating on high speed about 4 minutes more or until mixture forms stiff, glossy peaks (tips stand straight) and sugar dissolves. Pipe or spoon meringue over each chocolate kiss and onto the cookie base. Bake cookies in the 300° oven for 15 minutes or until meringue is lightly browned. Transfer to wire racks; cool. Makes 26 to 30 cookies.

Nutrition Facts per cookie: 89 calories, 5 g total fat (2 g saturated fat), 13 mg cholesterol, 31 mg sodium, 11 g carbohydrate, 0 g fiber, 1 g protein.

*Note: You can make the cookies up to this point and store, covered, for up to 3 days. Once meringue is added, cookies do not store well.

spider bites

prep: 30 minutes   **chill:** 2 hours   **bake:** 7 minutes   **oven:** 375°

You'll want many small hands helping you with these Halloween treats—they're as fun to make as they are to eat.

½ cup butter
¾ cup sugar
½ teaspoon baking powder
¼ teaspoon baking soda
¼ teaspoon salt
1 egg

2 ounces semisweet chocolate, melted
    and cooled
½ teaspoon vanilla
1⅓ cups all-purpose flour
½ cup miniature semisweet chocolate pieces
1 recipe Decorating Icing

1. In a medium mixing bowl beat the butter with an electric mixer on medium to high speed about 30 seconds. Add the sugar, baking powder, baking soda, and salt. Beat until combined. Beat in the egg, melted chocolate, and vanilla. Beat in as much of the flour as you can with the mixer. Stir in remaining flour and the chocolate pieces.

2. Shape dough into two 12-inch-long rolls. Wrap rolls in waxed paper; chill in the refrigerator at least 2 hours or up to 24 hours. Cut dough into ¼-inch-thick slices. Place slices 1 inch apart on an ungreased cookie sheet.

3. Bake cookies in a 375° oven about 7 minutes or until edges are set. Cool on cookie sheet for 1 minute. Transfer cookies to a wire rack; cool.

4. Spoon Decorating Icing into a decorating bag fitted with a writing tip or fluted tip. Pipe icing into various size spiders or other Halloween shapes on cookies. Let cookies stand until icing is set. Makes 90 cookies.

Decorating Icing: In a small mixing bowl stir together 1 cup sifted powdered sugar and enough milk to make an icing that is easy to pipe. Tint with desired colors of paste or liquid food coloring.

Nutrition Facts per cookie: 34 calories, 2 g total fat (1 g saturated fat), 5 mg cholesterol, 23 mg sodium, 5 g carbohydrate, 0 g fiber, 0 g protein.

spiced and iced pumpkin cookies

prep: 30 minutes   **bake:** 8 minutes   **oven:** 375°

Here's a pumpkin-flavored treat that you can keep in a cookie jar. Have this popular recipe on hand from October through Christmas for all of your holiday well-wishers.

1 cup shortening	¼ teaspoon baking soda
½ cup granulated sugar	1 egg
½ cup packed brown sugar	1 cup canned pumpkin
1½ teaspoons pumpkin pie spice	2 cups all-purpose flour
½ teaspoon baking powder	1 recipe Brown Sugar Glaze

1. In a medium mixing bowl beat shortening with an electric mixer on medium to high speed for 30 seconds. Add the granulated sugar, brown sugar, pumpkin pie spice, baking powder, and baking soda. Beat until combined, scraping sides of bowl. Beat in the egg and pumpkin. Beat in as much of the flour as you can with the mixer. Stir in remaining flour.

2. Drop dough by a rounded teaspoon 2 inches apart onto an ungreased cookie sheet. Bake cookies in a 375° oven for 8 to 10 minutes or until tops seem firm. Transfer cookies to a wire rack; cool. Spread cooled cookies with Brown Sugar Glaze. Makes 42 cookies.

Brown Sugar Glaze: In a small saucepan combine ½ cup packed brown sugar, 3 tablespoons butter, and 1 tablespoon milk. Heat and stir until butter melts. Remove saucepan from heat. Stir in 1 cup sifted powdered sugar and 1 teaspoon vanilla.

Nutrition Facts per cookie: 109 calories, 6 g total fat (2 g saturated fat), 7 mg cholesterol, 24 mg sodium, 14 g carbohydrate, 0 g fiber, 1 g protein.

how hot is hot?

Timing and temperature are important to baking. Be sure your oven is calibrated properly by checking it with an accurate thermometer. Check your thermometer first by immersing the end of it into a pot of boiling water. (Do not let thermometer sit on the bottom of the pot.) The thermometer should read 212°, the temperature at which water boils. Set your oven for 350°, allowing 10 minutes for it to reach a steady temperature. Place the thermometer in the oven; wait at least 5 minutes. If the thermometer reads differently from the set temperature, adjust the oven temperature up or down the number of degrees your oven is off. (For example, if the thermometer reads 360° when the oven is set at 350°, the oven is 10° too hot. So, to bake at 350°, you should set the oven at 340°.) If your oven is off by more than 50° you should have it serviced and tested by a qualified repair person.

hamantaschen

prep: 40 minutes   **chill:** 2 hours   **bake:** 10 minutes   **oven:** 350°

Purim, a festive Jewish holiday, is celebrated with prizes, noisemakers, costumes, and sweets. A gift of these cookies (pronounced HAH-mahn-tah-shuhn), which are shaped like miniature hats, is a time-honored tradition.

½ cup butter
¼ cup granulated sugar
¼ cup packed brown sugar
2 teaspoons baking powder
1 teaspoon vanilla
⅛ teaspoon salt

2 eggs
2 teaspoons finely shredded orange peel
¼ cup orange juice
2¾ cups all-purpose flour
½ cup cake and pastry filling, such as poppy
    seed, prune, apricot, or cherry

1. In a large mixing bowl beat the butter with an electric mixer on medium speed for 30 seconds. Add the granulated sugar, brown sugar, baking powder, vanilla, and salt, beating until light and fluffy. Beat in the eggs, 1 at a time, until well combined. Slowly add the shredded orange peel and orange juice (mixture may appear curdled). Beat in as much of the flour as you can with the mixer. Stir in the remaining flour. Cover and chill dough in the refrigerator about 2 hours or until easy to handle.

2. Divide dough in half. On a lightly floured surface, roll out 1 portion of the dough to ⅛-inch thickness. Using a fluted biscuit or cookie cutter, cut into 2¼- to 2½-inch circles, rerolling scraps as necessary. Brush edge of circles with water. Spoon ½ teaspoon of desired filling onto the center of each circle.

3. Bring 2 of the circle's opposite edges together toward the top to make a "V," and pull the unfolded edge up, pinching the edges together to form a shape like a three-cornered hat. Leave the center slightly open to expose filling. Place cookies on an ungreased cookie sheet.

4. Bake in a 350° oven for 10 to 12 minutes or until cookies are lightly browned. Transfer cookies to a wire rack; cool. Repeat with the remaining dough and filling. Makes about 60 cookies.

Nutrition Facts per cookie: 60 calories, 2 g total fat
(1 g saturated fat), 11 mg cholesterol, 37 mg sodium,
9 g carbohydrate, 0 g fiber, 1 g protein.

rugalach

prep: 45 minutes   **chill:** 2 hours   **bake:** 15 minutes   **oven:** 350°

Rugalach (pronounced RUHG-uh-luhkh), a rich cream cheese cookie, is a Hanukkah tradition. This recipe offers several variations to the classic date-filled or poppy-seed versions.

½ cup butter, softened
1 3-ounce package cream cheese, softened
1 tablespoon honey
1 cup all-purpose flour

1 recipe Cinnamon-Pecan Filling, Cranberry Filling, or Chocolate-Walnut Filling
1 cup sifted powdered sugar
¼ teaspoon vanilla
1 to 2 tablespoons milk

1. In a large mixing bowl beat the butter and cream cheese with an electric mixer on medium to high speed for 30 seconds. Beat in honey until combined. Beat in as much of the flour as you can with the mixer. Stir in remaining flour. Divide dough into 4 equal portions. Cover; chill dough in the refrigerator for at least 2 hours.

2. On a lightly floured surface, roll each portion of dough into a 6-inch circle. Sprinkle or spread about 2 tablespoons desired filling over each circle. Cut each circle into 8 wedges. Starting at the wide end, roll up each wedge. Place rolls, point down, about 2 inches apart on an ungreased cookie sheet. If desired, gently bend each roll to form a crescent.

3. Bake cookies in a 350° oven about 15 minutes or until golden brown. Transfer to a wire rack; cool.

4. Meanwhile, combine the powdered sugar, vanilla, and enough milk to make an icing of drizzling consistency. Drizzle over cooled crescents. Makes 32 cookies.

Cinnamon-Pecan Filling: In a small bowl combine ½ cup very finely chopped pecans, ¼ cup sugar, and ¾ teaspoon ground cinnamon.

Cranberry Filling: In a small bowl combine ¼ cup very finely chopped walnuts or pecans, ⅓ cup very finely chopped cranberries, 2 teaspoons honey, and ¼ teaspoon ground cinnamon.

Chocolate-Walnut Filling: In a small bowl combine ¼ cup very finely chopped walnuts, ¼ cup sugar, and ¼ cup miniature semisweet chocolate pieces.

Nutrition Facts per cookie with Cinnamon-Pecan Filling: 79 calories, 5 g total fat (2 g saturated fat), 11 mg cholesterol, 37 mg sodium, 8 g carbohydrate, 0 g fiber, 1 g protein.

best for

apple butter crescents

prep: 45 minutes **chill:** 3 hours **bake:** 8 minutes **oven:** 375°

The delicate flavor of apple butter gives these light and tender crescent cookies a sublime touch. For another time, try them with raspberry or peach jam.

⅔ cup butter
1 cup sugar
1 teaspoon baking powder
¼ teaspoon salt
2 eggs

1 teaspoon vanilla
3 cups all-purpose flour
⅔ cup apple butter or seedless raspberry jam
2 tablespoons sugar
½ teaspoon ground cinnamon

1. In a large mixing bowl beat butter with an electric mixer on medium to high speed for 30 seconds. Add the 1 cup sugar, the baking powder, and salt. Beat until combined, scraping sides of bowl occasionally. Beat in eggs and vanilla. Beat in as much of the flour as you can with the mixer. Stir in remaining flour. Divide dough in half. Cover; chill dough in refrigerator for 3 hours or until easy to handle.

2. Line cookie sheet with foil or parchment paper; set aside. On a lightly floured surface, roll half of the dough into a 12-inch square. Cut into sixteen 3-inch squares. Spread about 1 teaspoon apple butter or jam down the middle of each square. Fold 1 edge of the dough over the filling. Fold over the other edge (see photos, *opposite page*). Place on prepared cookie sheet. Make 3 cuts halfway through

dough on one long side of each cookie. Bend cookie slightly to separate cuts (see photo, *right*). Combine the 2 tablespoons sugar and the cinnamon; sprinkle cookies with some of the sugar-cinnamon mixture. Repeat with remaining dough, remaining filling, and remaining sugar-cinnamon mixture.

3. Bake in a 375° oven for 8 to 10 minutes or until golden brown. Transfer cookies to a wire rack; cool. Makes 32 cookies.

Nutrition Facts per cookie. 116 calories, 4 g total fat (2 g saturated fat), 24 mg cholesterol, 71 mg sodium, 18 g carbohydrate, 0 g fiber, 2 g protein.

guests

When guests are coming and you want to serve something

extra-special, turn to these company-worthy cookies.

two-tone biscotti

prep: 20 minutes   **bake:** 25 minutes/20 minutes   **oven:** 375°/325°   **cool:** 1 hour

Good biscotti are toothsome and crisp, benefiting from a generous dip in a hot cup of freshly brewed coffee. Here you get two distinct tastes—rich chocolate and delicate orange—in one cookie.

⅔ cup butter
1⅓ cups sugar
3 teaspoons baking powder
¼ teaspoon salt
4 eggs

1 teaspoon vanilla
4 cups all-purpose flour
1½ cups semisweet chocolate pieces, melted and cooled
1 cup finely chopped hazelnuts (filberts)
1 tablespoon finely shredded orange peel

1. In a large mixing bowl beat butter with an electric mixer on medium to high speed for 30 seconds. Add sugar, baking powder, and salt; beat until combined. Beat in eggs and vanilla. Beat in as much of the flour as you can with the mixer. Stir in remaining flour.

2. Divide dough in half. Place half in another bowl. Into half of the dough, stir the melted chocolate and ½ cup of the nuts. Into the other half of the dough, stir the orange peel and the remaining nuts.

3. Divide each half of dough into 3 portions. With lightly floured hands, shape each portion into a rope about 14 inches long. Place a rope of each color side by side on an ungreased cookie sheet. Twist ropes around each other several times. Flatten slightly to a 2-inch width. Repeat with the other ropes, placing twists about 4 inches apart on the cookie sheet.

4. Bake biscotti in a 375° oven about 25 minutes or until lightly browned. Cool on cookie sheet for 1 hour or until completely cool.

5. Transfer loaves to a cutting board. Cut each loaf crosswise into ½-inch-thick slices. Lay slices, cut side down, on the cookie sheet. Bake in a 325° oven for 10 minutes. Turn the slices over and bake 10 to 15 minutes more or until dry and crisp. Transfer cookies to a wire rack; cool. Makes about 70 biscotti.

Nutrition Facts per biscotti: 88 calories, 4 g total fat (1 g saturated fat), 14 mg cholesterol, 43 mg sodium, 10 g carbohydrate, 1 g fiber, 1 g protein.

cranberry-pecan tassies

prep: 45 minutes   **bake:** 30 minutes   **oven:** 325°

Fruit- and nut-filled tassies—old Scottish for "little cup"—dress up the after-dinner plate with their special-occasion flavor and homestyle comfort.

½ cup butter, softened	¾ cup packed brown sugar
1 3-ounce package cream cheese, softened	1 teaspoon vanilla
1 cup all-purpose flour	Dash salt
1 egg	⅓ cup finely chopped cranberries
	3 tablespoons chopped pecans

1. For pastry, in a mixing bowl beat the butter and cream cheese until combined. Stir in the flour. If desired, chill in refrigerator for 1 hour.

2. Shape the dough into 24 balls; place in ungreased 1¾-inch muffin pans. Press dough evenly against bottom and up sides of each muffin cup.

3. For the filling, in a mixing bowl beat together the egg, brown sugar, vanilla, and salt just until smooth. Stir in the cranberries and pecans. Spoon filling into the pastry-lined muffin cups.

4. Bake tassies in a 325° oven for 30 to 35 minutes or until pastry is golden brown. Cool in pans on wire racks. Remove from pans by running a knife around the edges. Makes 24 tassies.

Nutrition Facts per tassie: 94 calories, 6 g total fat (3 g saturated fat), 23 mg cholesterol, 59 mg sodium, 10 g carbohydrate, 0 g fiber, 1 g protein.

gourmet oatmeal cookies

prep: 25 minutes   **bake:** 13 minutes   **oven:** 350°

Oatmeal cookies get a cosmopolitan makeover with chocolate-covered raisins and chopped walnuts.

2 cups rolled oats
⅓ cup flaked coconut
⅓ cup butter
⅓ cup shortening
¾ cup granulated sugar
¾ cup packed brown sugar

1 teaspoon baking soda
2 eggs
1 teaspoon vanilla
1 cup all-purpose flour
1 cup coarsely chopped walnuts
1 cup chocolate-covered raisins

1. For oat flour, place ½ cup oats in a blender container or 1 cup in a food processor bowl. Cover and blend or process until oats turn into a powder. Transfer powder to a small bowl. Repeat with remaining oats, ½ to 1 cup at a time. Set aside.

2. Place coconut in blender container or food processor bowl. Cover and blend or process until coconut is very finely chopped. Set aside.

3. In a large mixing bowl beat butter and shortening with an electric mixer on medium to high speed for 30 seconds. Add the granulated sugar, brown sugar, and soda. Beat until combined, scraping sides of bowl occasionally. Beat in the eggs and vanilla. Beat in oat flour, coconut, and as much of the all-purpose flour as you can with the mixer. Stir in remaining flour. Stir in the walnuts and raisins.

4. Drop cookie dough by a ¼-cup measure about 4 inches apart onto an ungreased cookie sheet. Bake cookies in a 350° oven for 13 to 15 minutes or until the edges are golden brown. Cool on cookie sheet for 1 minute. Transfer the cookies to a wire rack; cool. Makes 15 large cookies.

To make standard size cookies: Drop the dough by a rounded teaspoon 2 inches apart on an ungreased cookie sheet. Bake in a 350° oven for 8 to 10 minutes or until the edges are lightly browned. Transfer cookies to a wire rack; cool. Makes 36 cookies.

Nutrition Facts per large cookie: 336 calories, 18 g total fat (6 g saturated fat), 41 mg cholesterol, 142 mg sodium, 42 g carbohydrate, 2 g fiber, 5 g protein.

lemon drops

prep: 25 minutes   **bake:** 8 minutes   **oven:** 375°

Break out the good china and serve these tangy, glazed cookies with hot lemon tea.

½ cup butter
¾ cup granulated sugar
 4 teaspoons grated lemon peel
½ teaspoon baking powder
½ teaspoon baking soda
⅛ teaspoon salt

1 egg
½ cup dairy sour cream
⅓ cup lemon juice
 2 cups all-purpose flour
 1 recipe Lemon Glaze

1. In a large mixing bowl beat butter with an electric mixer on medium to high speed for 30 seconds. Add the sugar, lemon peel, baking powder, baking soda, and salt. Beat until combined, scraping sides of bowl. Beat in egg, sour cream, and lemon juice. Beat in as much of the flour as you can with the mixer. Stir in remaining flour.

2. Drop dough by a slightly rounded tablespoon 3 inches apart on an ungreased cookie sheet. Bake cookies in a 375° oven about 8 minutes or until tops are firm.

Transfer the cookies to a wire rack. Brush the tops of warm cookies with Lemon Glaze; cool. Makes about 36 cookies.

Lemon Glaze: In a small mixing bowl stir together ¼ cup granulated sugar and 2 tablespoons lemon juice.

Nutrition Facts per cookie: 72 calories, 4 g total fat (1 g saturated fat), 11 mg cholesterol, 57 mg sodium, 9 g carbohydrate, 0 g fiber, 1 g protein.

easy substitutions

Help! You've already started making your cookies and you don't have a certain ingredient. Here are some suggestions to help you get by:

• 1 teaspoon baking powder: Use ½ teaspoon cream of tartar plus ¼ teaspoon baking soda.
• 1 cup sugar: Use 1 cup packed brown sugar.
• 1 cup dairy sour cream: Use 1 cup plain yogurt.
• 1 cup buttermilk: Use 1 tablespoon lemon juice or vinegar plus enough whole milk to make 1 cup (let stand for 5 minutes), or 1 cup whole milk plus 1¾ teaspoons cream of tartar, or 1 cup yogurt.
• 1 ounce semisweet chocolate: Use 1 square unsweetened chocolate plus 1 tablespoon sugar.
• 1 ounce unsweetened chocolate: Use 3 tablespoons unsweetened cocoa powder plus 1 tablespoon shortening or cooking oil.

index